MORE JOBS,
LESS INFLATION

More Jobs,
Less Inflation

The case for a counter-inflation tax

Richard Layard

GRANT
McINTYRE

First published in 1982 by Grant McIntyre Ltd
90/91 Great Russell Street London WC1B 3PY

British Library Cataloguing in Publication Data

Layard, Richard
　　More jobs, less inflation.
　　1.　Inflation (Finance) — Great Britain
　　I.　Title
　　332.4'1　　　　HG939.5

ISBN 0-86216-090-1
ISBN 0-86216-092-8 Pbk

Typeset in 11/13pt IBM Press Roman by
Cambrian Typesetters, Farnborough
Printed and bound in Great Britain by Billings, Worcester

Contents

Preface

There is hardly a thought in this book that has not been discussed with Richard Jackman, and there are many that have been profoundly influenced by David Grubb, James Meade and Stephen Nickell. I am extremely grateful to them, and also to Orley Ashenfelter, Jeremy Bray, Oliver Hart, Chris Huhne, John Kay, Abba Lerner and Chris Pissarides, and to many others who came to a conference on this topic in January 1982 financed by the Esmee Fairbairn Charitable Trust. The book was splendidly typed at lightning speed by Alan Hinchliffe and Bettie Jory.

Richard Layard

Centre for Labour Economics,
London School of Economics

May 1982

To Sally

Part I
The Proposal

1

The Problem

Europe faces mass unemployment. But why can governments apparently do nothing about it? The reason is simple. Inflation would rise if unemployment were reduced by normal methods. For unemployment is at present the main check on inflation. If we take away that check, we have to find another one. This is the main challenge facing economic thinkers in the world today.

INFLATION IS A PERMANENT PROBLEM

In facing this problem, we have to recognize two different sides to the inflation problem. One is how to reduce inflation, and the other is how eventually to keep it steady. Which of these is the more important? Many people are tempted to focus only on the first and to suppose that once inflation has been reduced, the job will have been done. Nothing could be less true. For we shall still be left with the problem of how to stop it rising again. The permanent problem is how to *contain* inflation. This is the central issue. Temporary policies to *reduce* inflation may be important. But they cannot solve the basic problem, which is how to have full employment on a permanent basis without having ever-increasing inflation.

THE IMPLICATIONS OF NOT HAVING AN INCOMES POLICY

There are basically only three ways to control inflation. One is to rely on high unemployment. This is the present Conservative route. In Britain we are surrounded by the costs of unemployment generated in order to reduce inflation. But the more important question is how much unemployment will be needed in future to stop inflation going up again. I estimate that we would need rather over 8 per cent, in other words over 2 million unemployed. This could only be acceptable if the costs of any alternative policy were so great as to exceed the benefits of reduced unemployment.

THE PROBLEMS OF A CENTRALIZED INCOMES POLICY

So what are the alternatives? One is a centrally regulated incomes policy of the traditional type. This is a possible route for the British Labour Party. It could be purely statutory (like the policy under Heath from 1972—74), or based on agreement with the unions (like the policy from 1975—77). But in either case it has three unacceptable features.

First, free collective bargaining is in effect suspended, since settlements have to conform to externally-imposed rules. People are willing to accept this kind of thing for a while, but eventually they rebel against external regulation of something which they consider a basic human right. This is the right to settle wages by bargaining between the employer and the worker. For this reason it is politically impossible and undesirable for a centrally regulated incomes policy to be permanent. And yet, as we have seen, it is essential to have a permanent incomes policy if we are to deal with the permanent problem of unemployment.

A second problem with conventional incomes policies is that, if they are to persist, they have to provide some mechanism for the adjustment of relativities. This mechanism is the ruling of a central body. But it is extremely difficult for any central body to get enough information to give sensible rulings on the thousands of cases that have to be decided. From reading the newspapers one is apt not to realize how many settlements there are. In Britain today two thirds of workers have their pay settled by bargaining with their individual employers.[1] An effective supervision of this number of settlements is virtually out of the question, except in a crude way for a short period.

Thirdly there is the problem of the link between settlements and actual pay. Clearly it is actual earnings paid out that determine the cost of labour and hence ultimately the prices in the shops. And yet it is now increasingly difficult for an outsider to tell how earnings will actually be affected by any particular settlement. This is because an increasing part of earnings consists of payments-by-results and other formulae. So incomes policies which are designed to bear on settlements may have only a limited impact on earnings. Thus, for three reasons, conventional incomes policies, though they may work for short periods of time, are not really feasible on a permanent basis.

A COUNTER-INFLATION TAX

This leaves us with the third possibility – an incomes policy that works by general incentives rather than by the regulation of individual cases. This means using the tax system to discourage an excessive growth of wages. This is not a new idea. It was first suggested by Wallich and Weintraub in the USA in 1971.[2] In Britain it has featured in the Liberal Party's approach to inflation for the past ten years.[3] Many detailed schemes have been put forward, and I shall discuss the various alternatives in due course. But the most promising approach seems to be as follows. Each year the government should declare a norm for the growth of average hourly earnings. If a firm controls the growth of its average hourly pay to this level, it is subject to no tax penalty. But if it goes above the norm, it pays a tax on all its excess wage payments. For example suppose the norm was 2 per cent and a firm paid a 5 per cent growth in average hourly earnings. It would be taxed on the 3 per cent difference. So if the tax rate was 100 per cent, the firms tax liability would equal roughly 3 per cent of its total wage bill (to be precise, 3/105th of it). To ensure that the average mark-up of prices over wages did not rise due to an increase in the total tax burden upon business as a whole, there would be an equivalent general cut in the rate of employers' National Insurance (social security) contributions.

Compare an arrangement like this with a centralized incomes policy. First, there is no absolute compulsion on anybody. Free collective bargaining continues. Firms and workers can agree on pay rises above the norm, but they are discouraged from going too far by the tax. If a group is paid above the norm, the policy has not broken down, nor is the policy or the government discredited. The tax can be imposed without the agreement of the unions. Though the government would discuss the policy with the unions, it could if necessary impose it without their agreement. So we have a policy that can be permanent. Second, the adjustment of relativities is determined in a decentralized manner through collective bargaining, and not by a central pay body. This should appeal to all those who believe that excessive centralism is one of the basic evils of our day. And finally the tax bears on actual pay and not on notional settlements.

So we have found a way of influencing incomes that does not suffer from the problems of a centralized incomes policy. We do not, thank God, have to accept mass unemployment as the only alternative.

2

How a Counter-Inflation Tax Would Work

EFFECTS ON UNEMPLOYMENT

How would the tax work? To think about this, we need to know the relation between inflation and unemployment. There is powerful evidence that in Britain (and most other countries) the tendency for inflation to increase depends on the level of unemployment.[4] For example, I estimate (*very* approximately) that if unemployment is higher by 1 per cent, the tendency for inflation to increase will be reduced by 1½ per cent a year. But unemployment has to be quite high to stop inflation increasing – probably at least 8 per cent.[5]

Thus the effect of unemployment on inflation is as shown in the first column (A) of Table 1. Chart 1 makes the same point in graphical form. As line A of that chart shows, inflation is stable at 8 per cent unemployment. But if unemployment is 6 per cent, inflation rises by 3 percentage points each year, and so on.

By introducing the tax we introduce an additional downward force on inflation. Suppose that at any given level of unemployment the tax reduced the tendency for inflation to rise by 3 percentage points. This would reduce the safe level of unemployment (when inflation was steady) by 2 percentage points. For without the tax 6 per cent unemployment would produce 3 per cent extra inflation each year, and this 3 per cent is now offset by the tax. Thus we could now have unemployment at 6 per cent rather than 8 per cent. I consider this a minimum estimate of what could be expected.

TABLE 1   Relation between the change in inflation and the
level of unemployment[5]

Unemployment rate	Annual change in inflation rate		
	(A) *Without tax*	*(B)* *With tax*	*(C)* *With tax and other measures*
4%	6%	3%	1½%
5%	4½%	1½%	0
6%	3%	0	−1½%
7%	1½%	−1½%	−3%
8%	0	−3%	−4½%
9%	−1½%	−4½%	−6%
10%	−3%	−6%	−7½%

The result is shown in column B of Table 1. It is also graphed in line B of Chart 1, emphasizing the point that the basic aim of the tax is to reduce the unemployment level consistent with steady inflation.[6] For in the long-run, the inflation rate cannot go on rising or falling indefinitely. So the key issue becomes the level of unemployment which will hold it constant. In the short-run, of course, things are different. If the opportunities open to the government improve by a shift from schedule A to schedule B, the government can either choose lower inflation at the same rate of unemployment or it can choose lower unemployment at the same level of inflation. Or it can have a mixture of the two.

HOW IT WORKS

Why will the tax reduce the tendency for inflation to rise? It will affect the behaviour of both firms and workers. Take firms first. Under the tax any firm that gives a £1 wage increase will lose not only the £1, but also £1 times the tax rate. If the tax rate were 100 per cent, it would lose £2. If

Chart 1   Unemployment and wage inflation

This shows how higher unemployment reduces the tendency for inflation to increase. A counter-inflation tax would reduce inflation at each level of unemployment and thus lower the safe level of unemployment.

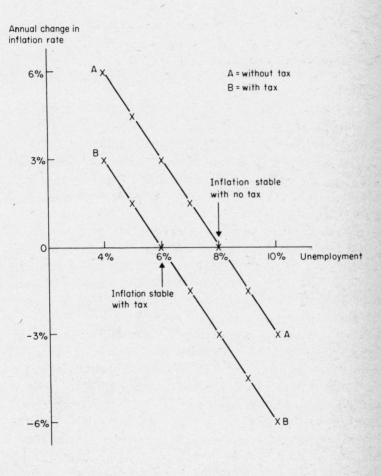

the tax rate were infinite, it would lose everything. This provides employers with a stronger incentive to resist wage claims. This is so even if other taxes are adjusted so that the employer with an average wage increase has no net increase in his tax burden. For the incentives facing the employer are now different.

This point is unaffected by the fact that the rate of National Insurance contributions has been reduced because of the expected proceeds of the tax on a nationwide basis. For that reduction is independent of the decision of any particular firm, whereas the firm's tax liability depends entirely on its own decisions. Suppose a firm has a £1,000,000 wage bill and £100,000 profits after tax. If the tax rate were 100 per cent, the firm could raise after-tax profits by £20,000 by holding pay to the norm instead of paying 2 per cent above it. It would surely take this point quite seriously.

The tax will also discourage workers from pushing wage claims as far as they would otherwise. For a union's wage claim is mainly limited by the fact that higher wages will reduce the employment of its members. Thus incomes policy should be designed so that a given wage increase for a group has a more adverse effect on the group's employment. This is exactly what the counter-inflation tax does. For employment depends on the employer's labour costs. And if wages increase by £1, the employer's cost of labour increases by £1 plus the tax rate. Hence a given increase in the unionists' pay packet is accompanied by a sharper fall in the demand for labour than if the tax were not there. For this reason unions will be more cautious in pushing their luck. In the economists' jargon the tax increases the elasticity of demand for labour. But union monopoly power depends entirely on the demand for labour being as inelastic as possible. Thus the tax effectively reduces the monopoly power of the unions.

It is important to note that if the scheme is made fiscally neutral a wage increase for one group will not reduce *total* employment, but it will reduce employment of the group concerned. Thus there is an incentive for the individual group to settle for lower wages.

This will do as a brief initial treatment of how the tax affects the incentives facing firms and workers. But we shall revert to this whole issue more rigorously in Chapter 7.

THE PUBLIC SECTOR

The counter-inflation tax would be confined to the private sector and the nationalized industries. Does this mean that it would have no effect in central and local government? Far from it. They would benefit from the tax in three important ways. First, if comparability is used as an argument in public sector pay settlements any scheme which helps in the private sector must contribute to the problem of public sector pay. This is crucial. There is a strong tendency to suppose that it is one or two settlements in the public sector (especially the miners') that somehow determine the national inflation rate. There is no evidence of this.[7] Broadly, private sector pay is determined by economic conditions in the private sector. Public sector pay follows private sector pay, but tends to get left behind in booms and under incomes policies, and then catches up again.[8]

Moreover, if private sector wages are held down by the tax, this will also restrain prices. And we know that the cost of living, as well as comparability, has an important influence on public sector pay.

Finally, an economy-wide norm would provide a useful frame of reference in public pay negotiations. In central and local government there could be a presumption that workers get the norm plus a catch-up equal to the difference between last year's private sector pay growth and last year's norm. (This formula could be modified to allow extra increases for government employees whose occupation was in shortage or whose comparator group had grown faster than the private sector average. Any extra payments of this type would of course be deducted when calculating the catch-up.) In this

way average pay in government and the private sector would
grow in line.[9] I discuss the problems of how to secure this
outcome further in Chapter 9.

In the nationalized industries the tax might have an
additional effect through the incentive which it provided
to employers to resist wage increases (just as in the private
sector). This incentive would obviously not hold if it was
known that the cash limit would be increased to pay the
tax, and doubtless this would sometimes occur. Thus it may
be that the tax would have little direct effect on miner's
pay. But it would profoundly affect all public pay (even
that of miners) through its effect on private sector wages
and prices.

THE INTRODUCTION OF THE TAX

Of course a key issue is how the tax is introduced, for this
will have a big effect on its credibility. For technical reasons
the tax could not come into force on the day it was announced. For it is a tax on wage growth, and can only be
levied once firms have been collecting data on appropriately-
defined wage payments for at least a year. This suggests the
following strategy. A government would simultaneously
announce a conventional incomes policy (say a percentage
limit on wage settlements) to last for, say, 18 months. It
would also announce that after 18 months this policy would
be replaced by a counter-inflation tax. When the 18 months
were up, the public would welcome the greater flexibility
to adjust differentials and redress anomalies that the tax
would permit. But they would also think of the counter-
inflation tax as a modification of a more familiar type of
incomes policy, which would add to the credibility of the
tax.

In fact the scheme should be quite popular. According to
the December 1978 issue of *Fortune* magazine, 58 per cent
of Americans believed in wage and price controls. It is true
that 54 per cent also believed in angels,[10] but this does not

invalidate the point that the public in Britain as well as in America would welcome some intervention on the wages front, especially if it were of an indirect kind that did not directly limit their own freedom to negotiate.

INCIDENCE: GAINERS AND LOSERS

It is natural to ask who gains and who loses from the tax. Clearly the unemployed gain from anything that increases employment. But would a counter-inflation tax also benefit those who already have work? A common left-wing argument against incomes policy is that it will lower the living standards of workers.

This need not be true. In Chapter 7 I assume that in the long term if private firms are to be induced to employ more people on a given set of equipment, profitability must be improved by a fall in wages relative to the firm's selling prices.[11] But does this mean that living standards have to fall? Not necessarily. For there are two other elements to be considered.

First, if the level of economic activity is higher, the level of investment will be higher. This will increase the stock of productive capital. And this in turn will raise the level of wages (relative to selling prices) at which it is profitable to employ any given number of workers. So there is no reason why the real wage that prevails in the medium term should be lower when unemployment is reduced.

In addition living standards depend not on the 'real product wage' but on the real product wage adjusted for the deduction of income tax and the effect of indirect taxes in pushing consumer prices above the firms' selling prices. Even if wages do fall relative to firms' selling prices, living standards can rise if taxes are cut. But this is exactly what a rise in employment permits, by increasing the tax base. A given government expenditure can now be financed with lower tax rates. This effect alone might be sufficient to ensure that living standards are maintained.[12] So workers have little to fear from a counter-inflation tax (or indeed any other form of incomes policy) in the medium and long run. In the short run the government might cut indirect taxes to maintain living standards, and thus make the policy more acceptable. But it is essential to have a policy which can, if necessary, be implemented without union agreement. It would be intolerable if union leaders could once again force a government to use unemployment as the only available defence against inflation.

3

Administration: A Bureaucratic Nightmare?

It is said that the US Internal Revenue Service commissioned a computer study of the words on the tax form that taxpayers most disliked. The computer found the most hated words to be spouse and Internal Revenue Service. Any tax is bound to be unpopular and one would certainly not suggest one unless one were confident that the benefits would exceed the cost. In any given economic environment both firms and workers would doubtless prefer to be rid of the tax. But the whole point of the tax is of course to change the environment: to face firms with a stronger demand for their products and workers with a better prospect of jobs. They should welcome the tax if they realized this.

But is a tax of this kind administratively feasible? When I first thought about this question, I thought that a counter-inflation tax might be quite difficult to administer. Happily, further study has shown that it can be relatively straight-foward. If you are willing to take this on trust, you can pass to Chapter 4. But, if not, please scrutinize the following proposals.

METHOD OF COLLECTION

First, the method of collection. The tax would be paid to the Inland Revenue once a quarter. Each firm would calculate its own liability, as it does with Pay As You Earn Income Tax (PAYE) and National Insurance (NI) contributions. It would then just send off a cheque to the relevant computer centre. It would also complete a brief proforma giving total earnings and man-hours, in justification of its assessed liability.

Firms have of course an incentive to lie over this tax, as they do over PAYE and NI payments. They would therefore be subject to spot audit at one week's notice (as with PAYE and NI). At present the audit of the whole of PAYE and NI at the firm's end requires under 500 inspectors, so there is no reason why the audit of the inflation tax should require more than 100 or so. Apart from a small amount of additional work at the two computer centres and the cost of designing the tax, this would be the total additional administrative cost to the Revenue.

COVERAGE

Next, the coverage of the tax. In the private sector it could be confined to companies employing over 100 workers. This would mean that under 20,000 companies were involved, compared with nearly a million pay-points for PAYE. This would save greatly on administrative cost both to the Revenue and to firms. Most of the firms affected have computerized payrolls, and record the clock hours of their hourly paid workers in a mechanical fashion. Moreover, in large firms cheating is less likely both because firms value their reputations, and because a manager who cheated would be less likely to gain personally from the firm's cheating.

One might think at first blush that if small firms were exempt this would lead to everyone wanting to become a small firm. But this would not happen provided that whatever adjustment was made to National Insurance applied only to firms which were liable for the counter-inflation tax.

THE TAX FORMULA

It is time now to look more closely at the tax formula. The first issue is whether firms should only be penalized for paying above the norm or also rewarded for paying below it. If firms which pay below the norm in any quarter get no credit for it in the form of a negative tax, then the tax penalizes those firms where wages grow in jumps relative to those with the same long-run wage growth but with a steadier growth path (the same would be true of a tax levied at an increasing marginal rate.) To prevent this one would need to have a negative range of tax, within which slow wage growth is rewarded But this would be more difficult for the Revenue to administer. It could also lead to complaints from workers that their firms were being rewarded for underpaying them. Whether a negative wage of tax is or is not desirable involves a delicate political judgement, but it is probably best to do without it.

The next issue is the appropriate level of the tax rate. It would need to be quite high, because we are taxing the annual *growth* of earnings. This means that if wages are raised this year, the tax paid on a *given wage level* next year is reduced (because next year's wage growth is reduced by an increase in this year's wage growth). This somewhat blunts the impact of the tax. But, to restore the sharpness of the tax, one can always increase the tax rate. The alternative is to have the tax liability relating to a fixed base. For example one could say that until further notice the tax will be levied on the excess of wages over their level when the tax was first announced. At some point the base would have to be changed, but if this was done in an unpredictable way this would discourage firms from thinking that they could derive any future tax benefit from a current wage increase. However a fixed base procedure would after a time heavily penalize firms that had upgraded their skill level; and it would also add to the complexity of taxing 'new' firms. So it could only be followed for a few years — at most the duration of a Parliament. I doubt whether such a Draconian policy would be desirable, and am inclined to favour a tax on annual wage growth levied at a high tax rate, of at least 100 per cent.

How would the norm be set? It should of course be discussed with the TUC and CBI but it would ultimately be the government's responsibility, as are all taxes. The level of the norm would be a matter of judgement. One would hope that after a period when the norm was steadily reduced it could ultimately be held fairly steady, with price inflation rather than wage inflation varying to reflect changes in the price of imports relative to domestic costs.

Two more technical points. The growth of hourly earnings would be calculated over the corresponding quarter in the previous year. This would ensure that a firm's tax liability was similar in each quarter of the year, rather than being concentrated in the quarters when settlements come into force. Like the Petroleum Revenue Tax, the Development Land Tax and the windfall profits tax on banks, this tax should not be allowable against corporation tax. For, if it were, its impact would be very different on those firms which do and those which do not pay corporation tax. About half of all workers are in firms which do not pay corporation tax, due to lack of taxable profit. For this reason too it would be no good following the original Wallich-Weintraub suggestion that the tax penalty on firms should be in the form of a rate of corporation tax that varied with the rate of wage increase.

MEASUREMENT OF EARNINGS

We now have to define the tax base. We want it to be hourly earnings. So how are we to measure earnings, and hours? The ideal definition of earnings would include all labour costs, including employers' and workers' pension contributions, as well as fringe benefits. However even if we could measure all these, there would be a problem. For employers can choose whether their workers' earnings-related pension arrangements will be covered by their own pension scheme or by the state scheme financed by full-rate National Insurance contributions. So if we included employers' pension contributions in labour cost, we should logically have to include their National Insurance contributions as well. This would soon give rise to cries of double taxation.

For this reason one is reasonably happy to take the simple route of defining earnings as those earnings that are liable for PAYE income tax. This excludes not only employers' but workers' pension contributions. As regards workers' contributions, firms are unlikely to increase these artificially in order to reduce tax liability.

It would be impracticable to include any fringe benefits not included in PAYE earnings. But if fringe benefits do increase relative to PAYE earnings, it is hard to see how in any one year, fringe-inclusive earnings growth could exceed fringe-exclusive growth by more than a fraction of 1 percentage point. For example the Treasury calculate that for those non-manual workers with whose pay the Civil Service is comparable, real income increased between 1975 and 1980 by ½ per cent a year due to increases in real fringe benefits. If manual workers were included the figure would be a good deal smaller. Moreover the period covered included an extremely severe incomes policy, and there are limits to the feasible growth of fringe benefits — the first £-worth is likely to be valued more highly by workers than the second £-worth.

MEASUREMENT OF HOURS

The need to measure hours is the biggest administrative problem faced by the tax. Unfortunately, measurement is essential since weekly earnings per worker would not do as a tax base. For a firm could easily reduce weekly earnings per worker by replacing full-time staff by part-time, and reducing overtime. While work-sharing of this kind might be desirable up to a point, it would make it easy for a firm to escape the tax, even though hourly pay went up sharply. Since it is hourly pay which determines the unit costs of the goods in the shops, the whole object of the exercise would have been aborted.

But it is not impossible to measure hours in a satisfactory way. For the 90 per cent (or so) of workers whose pay is time related there is no major difficulty. Hours would be hours worked (clock hours). For workers whose pay is time related, hours worked are recorded by nearly all firms. This applies to piece workers, as well as workers on straight time rates.

The next category of workers is those with contractual hours which are fixed. Here the main variation of hours worked comes through sickness, absence and changes in holidays. Sickness (and other) paid absence could be disregarded. Firms could be asked to attribute to a worker in each quarter one quarter of the annual hours he would work if he had his full quota of holidays and no sickness or other absence.

Finally, there are workers with no contractual hours — above all salesmen, but also many managers, academics and so on. Here the employer could be asked to put in whatever approximate figure he considered most appropriate. The exact figure would not matter greatly, provided it was not arbitrarily altered from year to year. To exclude workers working a small number of hours it might be wise to exclude from the measurement of earnings and hours all workers not liable for National Insurance contributions.

To monitor what was happening, firms would be required to submit with their tax cheque a statement of earnings, number of employees and assessed man-hours, separately for the three categories of employee. The Revenue would only accept an increase in contractual hours for non-time-paid staff where a satisfactory explanation was provided by the firm. For hourly paid workers, a firm that greatly increased its hours per worker would be a likely candidate for audit. It would also be a good idea if company accounts were required to include a statement of man-hours.

Thus it should be possible to handle the problem of hours. If it caused difficulties in the early stages of the tax, one could perhaps start off with a tax based on the average weekly earnings of full-time workers.[13] This would get round the problem of part-time workers, but would still discourage overtime more than might be desirable in the long term.

IDENTITY OF FIRMS

The tax would be levied on each firm taken as a whole.[14]
Totally new firms would be excluded. But there are obviously
problems connected with mergers and disintegration of firms.
These can be handled provided it is understood that wherever
there has been continuous economic activity that activity is
deemed to have a past. Thus with a merger, the present firm
would be treated as if in the previous year it had consisted of
its component firms. And if a firm disintegrated, its present
constituents would be treated as if they were a single firm.
(The allocation of liability would be a required topic in a
distingegration agreement.)

There are doubtless many ways in which firms will try to
evade the tax, some of which will come up in the next chapter.
But this is true of all taxes. People tend to assume that the
taxes we already have are securely founded, while any new
ones are insecure in the extreme. But, when one looks into
it, it seems that a counter-inflation tax could be quite straight-
forward. The bureaucratic nightmare would be a prolonged
period of conventional incomes policy.

4

Problems

So far I have praised the tax. The time has come to face up to the problems involved. But these problems must always be seen in perspective. In later life Maurice Chevalier was asked what he thought of old age. 'It's not so bad,' he replied, 'when you consider the alternative.'

The alternative to a counter-inflation tax is at least 2 per cent more of the work force unemployed (see Table 1). This means a loss of at least £5,000,000,000 of output, plus untold human suffering and degradation. So when one considers the inevitable costs of any kind of intervention, one must weigh them against the very major benefits.

In what follows I shall consider a whole range of problems, starting for the sake of honesty with the most serious.

WILL THE TAX DISCOURAGE EFFICIENCY?

The firms which pay the heaviest tax will be those whose wages rise the most. These will on the whole be those most able to pay the tax. But they will also be those where there is a need for wages to grow most rapidly, either to attract more labour or to buy out a restrictive manning practice. Let us look at these two cases in turn.

Some firms need to increase their relative wages to attract more labour. But this mainly happens when there is reasonably full employment. Thus this problem mainly arises where there is the major benefit of full employment itself to be set against the efficiency cost of the tax on adjustment.

A more serious problem is the discouragement of the

'productivity deal'. However before going into this problem, let me first dispel a few cobwebs. Productivity growth itself does not depend on workers in high productivity growth industries receiving higher wage increases than those in lower productivity growth industries. Quite the contrary. In general wages do not, and should not, grow faster in higher productivity growth industries. For it is only if wages grow fast in low productivity sectors as well that employers in these sectors will be forced to face the true cost of retaining labour. So wages rise at a similar rate in all sectors but prices grow at very different rates – much faster in the slow productivity growth sectors (haircuts) than in the high productivity growth sectors (electronics). In this way the fruits of high productivity growth ultimately get passed out to all the citizens *via* lower prices.

Of course this does not always happen at once, and there are certainly high productivity growth sectors where the net output per worker grows rapidly even when the cost of capital has been subtracted from it. Such firms are not passing on the fruits of technical progress to their customers as much as efficiency might require. But, given that, they may wish to boost morale by sharing the fruits with their work force. This is all right and the tax does not prevent them sharing out the cake in whatever way they consider fair. It merely reduces the size of the cake, but this should not cause major distortions since we are basically considering the distribution of the fruits of monopoly.

Much more serious is the problem of the true 'productivity' deal where it is a change in working practices, rather than new capital equipment, which raises the output per worker. Such changes are vital in Britain, and it would be very desirable if one could modify the tax in such a way that they were not discouraged. A possible arrangement would be this. Any firm that negotiated such a deal could notify the Revenue at the beginning of the year. During the year it would pay the tax. At the end of the year, it would record its achieved increase in productivity and calculate what part of it was due to the change in manning practice. It could then apply retro- spectively to the Revenue for a refund on any tax attributable to wages paid for better practices leading to higher produc- tivity. This is the best I have been able to think of, but I doubt if it is good enough. It is doubtful whether one *can* separate out these components of pay. The Revenue's rulings could cause ill-feeling and it is probably better to proceed with the blanket rule of no exceptions, and accept the efficiency costs. However any suggestions are welcome. One should stress of course that the tax is only paid in the year of the wage growth and not for ever: there is no permanent tax on this year's productivity deal.

I have been fairly apologetic so far about the way in which the tax would penalize the upward adjustment of differentials. Let me end this discussion with a comeback. Many of the adjustments in differentials which occur are not functional, along the lines I have been describing, but dysfunctional. They reflect temporary fluctuations, which are rapidly reversed in the following year or two. This demoralizes the temporary losers more than it satisfies the temporary gainers. To illustrate this let me mention two facts. If you take the dispersion of annual earnings increases across bargaining groups year by year, and compare this with the dispersion of average annual earnings increases averaged over the 10 years 1970–80, the year to year dispersion was on average five times higher than the long-run dispersion.[15] In other words most short-run changes in relativities got reversed soon after. I infer that about 4/5 of the short-run adjustment of relativities may have been dysfunctional. Moreover, as you would expect, the year to year dispersion has tended to be higher, the higher the level of inflation. Low inflation, especially when linked to an incomes policy, tends to reduce the amount of pointless change in relativities. So it is not by any means all bad that the counter-inflation tax will tend to reduce the rate of change of differentials.

Reverting to the wider question of efficiency, the tax will introduce a second type of distortion. With any given pattern of differentials, a firm can escape tax by increasing the proportion of unskilled workers in its work force. For example if an individual is paid £5,000 and the firm's average wage is £7,500, the firm can by hiring him reduce the tax by the difference (£2,500) times the tax rate.[16] The calculation exaggerates the inducement to hire unskilled workers since the effective subsidy is only paid in the year when the hiring is made and needs to be discounted suitably if we are asking whether the firm will make a permanent adjustment to its manning pattern. I estimate that the effective annual subsidy to unskilled labour would be very roughly £250 a year – or 5 per cent of the wage.[17] This does not seem to be a major distortion, and many people would think such a subsidy to unskilled labour a good thing. For if the high rate of unskilled unemployment is partly due to unskilled wages being above their market-clearing level, a subsidy of this kind can actually improve efficiency by offsetting the prior distortion. But a firm which has a particular need to upgrade its work force will certainly be penalized.

Another response a firm might make would be to sub-contract some of its skilled work to former employees becoming self-employed and forming small partnerships. Again the tax avoided by dis-employing a skilled worker paid say £10,000 is the difference from the average wage (again say £2,500) times the tax rate. This too must be discounted.

So let us round off our discussion of the efficiency costs of the tax. We have seen that there could be important costs, especially through the discouragement of productivity deals and the penalizing of firms upgrading their work-forces relative to the national average. But against these costs have to be set the benefits, which are also straight efficiency items. If the economy can be run at a 2 per cent higher level of output and this introduces distortions reducing output by ½ per cent, then the economy is more efficient to the tune of 1½ per cent of national income. This seems to me a minimum estimate of what is likely.

WHY NOT ATTACK UNION POWER DIRECTLY?

Some people, however, would argue that the same benefits could be got by a direct attack on union power, rather than by the indirect approach of a counter-inflation tax.[18] After all, the long-run excess supply of labour is caused basically by the unions forcing up real wages above the market-clearing level, as I too argue in Chapter 7. So why not (the argument goes) remove from the unions the legal powers which give them their monopoly power?

At first sight this may seem a plausible argument, and there are certainly important ways in which the legal power of unions should be reduced. But there are two basic points. First, institutional reform will be a long process and we cannot in the meantime just sit back and accept a 12 per cent unemployment rate. We must quickly establish a bulwark to hold inflation down while we reflate. But, secondly, institutional reform will always be limited by what are considered basic human rights. A perfectly competitive labour market would be one in which it was illegal for workers to combine in withdrawing their labour. But it is unthinkable to abolish the right to strike, since it is bound up with basic ideas of human dignity. So there are severe limits on the extent to which union power can be reduced.

It is therefore natural to use a tax as an additional weapon. One reason why this makes sense is that there is considerable respect for the laws of tax. There might be less respect for a burst of new laws explicitly directed against union power. I have no doubt that new laws *are* needed to control union power, but they will take time.

WHY NOT TAX WORKERS RATHER THAN FIRMS?

However if unions are the problem, one might at least consider levying the tax on workers, who are causing the problem, rather than on firms, which are trying to resist them.[19] In the formal economic analysis of Chapter 7, it does not matter which side is taxed, but this assumes that workers fully understand how the tax will affect the firm's ability to provide jobs. In practice workers lack this perception, which is why the tax would be more effective if it could be levied on workers (or even half on workers and half on firms). This would not be particularly difficult from an administrative point of view. One would not of course tax the individual worker on the basis of his or her individual increase in earnings. For that would involve taxing increases earned by promotion, by moves up the scale and so on. But one could with little difficulty compute the increase in average earnings in the firm where the worker was employed, and then tax all workers in the firm on the basis of the firm's increase in wage payments.

However if the tax was levied on workers, there could be major political opposition. If this opposition were strong enough, the policy would be abandoned and the whole search for a permanent solution would have failed. So it seems wisest to think in terms of a tax on firms.[20]

WHY NOT CONTROL PRICES?

One might argue that if the aim is to control inflation one should not bother about wages at all but should rather control prices. In fact the original proposal for a tax on inflation was for a tax on price increases. But there are major problems with direct controls on prices. First, it is very difficult to measure prices when the quality of the product can be changed and when new products are constantly coming into existence. These problems are much less severe with different qualities of labour. Second, as we have seen, the prices of different goods grow (and should grow) at very different rates, whereas the wages of different types of worker grow (and should grow) at fairly similar rates. So one could not contemplate any policy that treated all price increases on the same lines. This forces one back on a policy which allows goods to be priced so as to maintain a reasonable profit margin. But what is 'reasonable'? In the late 1970s the rule was the margin prevailing in the best 3 of the last 5 years. Even with such a procedure there is endless room for argument over the measurement of profit, depending on the treatment of capital cost. Price control is thus bound to involve a major bureaucratic apparatus. If it is effective, control on margins may in many cases discourage investment. But it will equally often be ineffective. Many firms would argue that under it they push up their prices faster than they otherwise would, in order to establish a nice high base in case the next bureaucrat next year is tougher than this year's bureaucrat.

So any attempt to control prices is either likely to be inefficient or ineffective. It seems best to keep clear of it. Moreover because of the difficulties of measurement, a price code is not likely to be a very good method of enforcing regulations on wages.

But if we control wages directly we *are* also controlling price inflation. For the long run growth of prices will be the same as of wages (apart from productivity change, terms of trade change and changes in distributional shares). Anyone who puts about figures showing that wages and prices over some short term have moved very differently (due for example to exchange rate changes) is simply trying to confuse people. The long-run growth of prices is primarily determined by the long-run growth of domestic costs, which mainly means wages.

WHAT ABOUT DIVIDENDS?

But even if prices cannot be controlled, should income from capital be left untouched? If high unemployment results from bad features of the labour market, there is no obvious reason to tamper with the capital market. On the other hand it is politically difficult to impose controls on wages and leave capital income untouched. The natural solution would be to have a tax on increases in dividends, levied on firms. There could be the same norm for dividend increases as for wage increases, and the same tax rate on increases above the norm. There would also of course have to be a share-out of the tax proceeds — perhaps most simply again *via* National Insurance.

There would of course be complaints that reinvested profits were exempt from control. However these are only of distributional significance if there are corresponding capital gains accruing to households; and the share of real capital gains in household income is rather small these days. In any case capital gains can be handled by a proper capital gains tax, integrated with the income tax.

WHAT ABOUT LOW PAY?

Some people believe that the main argument for incomes policy is that it enables you to kill two birds with one stone — to control inflation and to alter the structure of pay to help those who are worst off. But unfortunately one stone aimed at two birds often misses both. The inclusion of the flat rate element in the policy of 1975—76 set up tensions which helped to destroy incomes policy later in the 1970s. And it did little to redistribute income. But, more important, the connection between family poverty and low pay is not particularly close. So it is much better to deal with poverty through the Budget than through wages policy. I shall expand on this important argument in Chapter 8.

This brings us to the end of our list of problems. Some of the problems have to be endured for the sake of the greater good, while others can be solved by other methods. Unfortunately life is full of problems, and solving one creates others. But it is worth trying to solve the unemployment problem, even if it spawns some other local difficulties.

Part II
Supporting Analysis

5

The Causes of Unemployment in the Long Term

Behind the argument so far has lain a theory about the causes of unemployment. It is important to go into this, for, unless we have some idea of why unemployment is what it is, we can hardly hope to reduce it. Nor can we know how much we can reduce it by: could we get it down to 3 per cent (as in the 1960s) or only to, say, 7 per cent?

We have to distinguish at once between two issues. The first is what determines the level of unemployment at which inflation is held steady (the 8 per cent of Table 1). We shall follow Tobin in calling this 'safe' level NAIRU — the non-accelerating-inflation rate of unemployment. The second issue is what determines the actual level of unemployment. This can obviously deviate from the NAIRU (the 8 per cent figure) for some considerable time but not indefinitely.

For our present purposes the first issue is the main one, since this is what creates the permanent problem to which we are looking for a permanent solution. We shall consider it in this chapter. But the second question is also important, since it explains where we are today. We shall come to it in the next chapter.

UNEMPLOYMENT IN THE LONG RUN

As Chart 2 shows, there has been a long-term upward trend in unemployment since the early 1960s. At the same time inflation has not tended to fall. So there must have been a

Chart 2
Some recent British history[21]

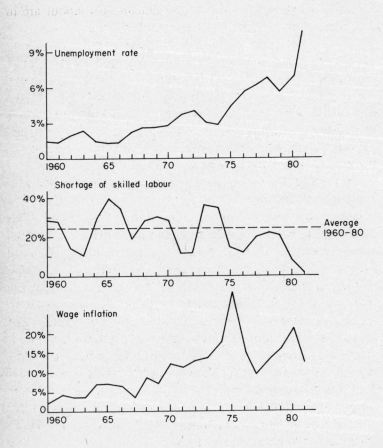

steady increase in the NAIRU. What could explain this upward trend?

There are rival ways of explaining the long-run level of unemployment. One is to say that it corresponds to an equilibrium where the supply and demand for labour are in equilibrium, apart from some inevitable frictional unemployment due to the time taken to match workers to jobs. This view is much favoured in the USA. The equilibrium level of unemployment would of course vary with the level of social security benefits, since the more generous they are the less the inducement to work. Since, as we shall see, unemployment benefits became more easily available over most of the period, this might seem to provide a complete explanation of the growth in unemployment.

This approach is what might be called the 'supply-side' explanation of unemployment. It relies on the idea that fewer of the unemployed are effectively supplying their labour in the market. Evidence in support of this explanation comes from the fact that the numbers of unemployed at any particular level of labour shortage have increased greatly. This is illustrated in Chart 3. This chart takes the data from the first two rows of Chart 2 and plots them against each other. As one would expect there is a tendency for unemployment to rise when employers find it easier to get labour (as for example between 1975 and 1976). But the remarkable thing is that comparing the 1970s with the 1960s unemployment was much higher even when labour was in equally short supply. For example unemployment in 1976 was over double what it was in 1963, even though employers found it if anything harder to get labour in 1976.

These extra people unemployed must almost by definition have not been really available for work. For otherwise vacancies would have been reduced. I say 'almost by definition' since this would not hold if there had been an increasing mismatch of workers and jobs. In such a case there might be more workers available per vacancy but having the wrong skills or located in the wrong part of the country. This possibility can be investigated by looking at the dispersion of the ratio of unemployed people to vacancies, measured across occupations or regions. There is no evidence of growing dispersion,[22] and hence no evidence of growing 'mismatch'. So we have clear evidence that unemployment has risen in part due to a 'supply-side' increase in the number of unemployed people not in some sense available for work. Later on I shall explain why this has occurred.

But the key point for our present argument is that this is *not the only thing* that has happened. There has been a second change of profound importance. According to the 'equilibrium' approach we have been following so far, one would, in the absence of any change in mismatch, expect the average level of labour shortage to be similar when one business cycle is compared with another. Yet, comparing the period from 1975 onwards with the entire period, the level of labour shortage has never even reached its previous long-run average. According to equilibrium theory it should be the shortage of labour that drives up inflation. Yet over the period since 1976 wage inflation has not fallen. It is in fact now about the same as it was in 1976/7.

So evidently it now requires less shortage of labour to contain inflation than it used to. The same is true in Europe. As Chart 4 shows, the same pattern of low vacancies (and low capacity utilization) has prevailed in the EEC. How can this be? We clearly cannot explain it in terms of the equilibrium approach. Instead we must take into account the target levels of real wages which workers are aiming at in their wage settlements. The simplest model is one where we think of unions as setting wages so as to do the best for their members after taking into account the employment consequences of the wage settlement. I shall outline such a model later, and also explain why the unions have now chosen a real wage and a level of employment which leaves the labour market much slacker than before.

Chart 3
Unemployment and labour shortage in Britain

This shows for each year the level of unemployment and the level of labour shortage. At any level of labour shortage (or job availability) the numbers unemployed have steadily increased.

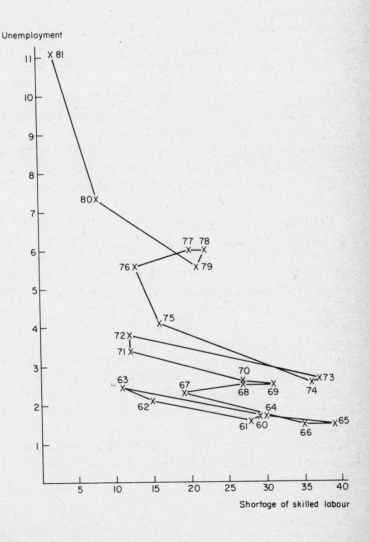

Shortage of skilled labour

Chart 4
Some recent history in the EEC[23]

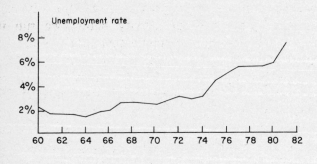

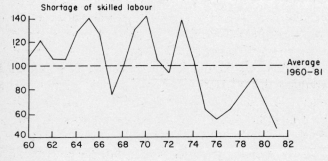

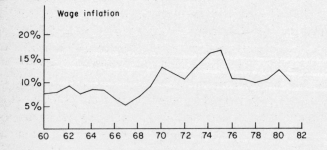

THE ATTAINABLE LEVEL OF UNEMPLOYMENT

But for the present I want to emphasize that this post-1975 slack in the labour market gives us scope for achieving a permanently higher level of activity before we run into shortages of labour supply. Suppose that with the aid of the counter-inflation tax, we could run the economy at the average level of tightness (measured by labour shortage) experienced in the 1960s. How much less unemployment would correspond to the tightening of the market? We can answer this question by looking at the relation between labour shortage and unemployment, and then seeing how unemployment would fall if labour shortage was increased by the stipulated amount. The answer is that we could simply on that account get the NAIRU down by nearly 2 percentage points.[24] But we could do a good deal better than that. On top of the inflation tax, we should adopt a number of other measures to reduce the NAIRU. First, we should administer social security with a much stricter work test. This can only be done when the labour market is reasonably tight, but there is no reason why with the level of vacancies that prevailed in 1978 a stricter work test could not have been enforced. Second, we need income maintenance policies that encourage work. This does not mean cutting social security for the unemployed but improving support for poor families in work. This requires a much more generous and consolidated means-tested benefit, which could ultimately (once the income tax is computerized) be paid out automatically in the worker's pay packet.[25] Third, we need policies which will direct labour demand from tight markets into those which are slacker, due to wage rigidities of one kind or another. These measures include subsidies for youth employment and for additional jobs in high unemployment regions. And finally we need to train our workers so as to shift them out of the over-supplied markets for unskilled labour into the tighter market for skills.

I shall discuss these various policies more fully in Chapter 10. With their aid I see no reason why we could not reduce the NAIRU to 5 per cent. After all, we had 5½–6 per cent from 1976 to 1978 without disastrous results, though helped by an incomes policy. But to aim at less than 5 per cent unemployment without a war seems rather optimistic.

THE CAUSES OF SUPPLY-SIDE UNEMPLOYMENT

I have asserted that social security plays an important role in explaining the growth of unemployment at any given level of vacancies. I should produce some evidence of this. In the nature of things the evidence cannot be conclusive.

There are two dimensions to social security – the money available and the terms on which the money is available. I believe the second matters most, but let us start with the money. Chart 5 shows in Panel A the supplementary benefit level for a single person. This is probably the most relevant category of person since about a half of unemployed men are single, and only a quarter have children.[26] Supplementary benefit is the most relevant rate since in 1978 53 per cent of unemployed men had their income level determined by supplementary benefit, compared with only 30 per cent by unemployment benefit.[27] As the Chart shows, the level of benefits relative to income in work rose up to 1967 and has remained roughly constant since then, with a slight fall in recent years.

My colleague Stephen Nickell has compared unemployed people with different ratios of benefit to income in work. He finds that, other things equal, unemployment duration goes up by roughly 1 per cent for each 1 per cent increase in the benefit ratio.[28] Assuming some lag in the response of unemployment, the increases in the ratio in the early and mid 1960s could explain some of the increases in unemployment up to the early 1970s, but nothing like all of it. But perhaps we should also take into account the real value of benefits (relative to the Retail Price Index) shown in Panel B. Even

Chart 5
Supplementary benefit for a single person[29]

Panel A: As a percentage of the net income of someone on average male earnings
Panel B: Relative to the Retail Price Index (value at 1980 prices)

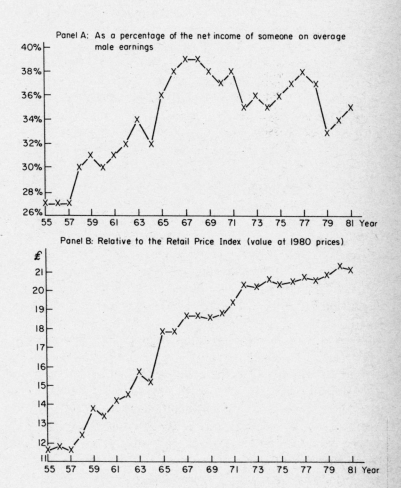

Panel A: As a percentage of the net income of someone on average male earnings

Panel B: Relative to the Retail Price Index (value at 1980 prices)

in the 1970s this continued to rise. According to Nickell's results this would have no effect since income in work rose at the same rate. However it does seem reasonable to suppose it had some effect, which could have continued well into the 1970s. But again it cannot explain much of the increase in unemployment in the 1970s.

I attach more importance to the terms on which benefits have been available. I refer to the informal changes in the administration of social security, whereby throughout the sixties and seventies less and less pressure was put upon the unemployed to find work. It is extremely difficult to get hard evidence on this. I have however assembled data on the frequency with which unemployed people are refused social security (see Table 2). Such evidence can hardly be decisive, but it does at any rate add a dimension to the story.

Let us start with the denial of benefit. If a person on unemployment benefit refuses an offer of suitable employment or 'neglects to avail' of opportunities of work that exist, the employment service can refer his case to an insurance officer. If the officer accepts the charge, then (subject to appeal) the person loses his unemployment benefit for up to six weeks. As the table shows, the numbers referred fell steadily up to 1973 after which they fell precipitously. In addition, from 1974 onwards there was a sharp fall in the proportion of all referred people who were eventually refused benefit.

However a person who is disqualified from unemployment benefit can still get some supplementary benefit. Normally any individual whose income is below the national minimum gets supplementary benefit sufficient to raise him to the minimum. But if he has been disqualified from unemployment benefit he loses 40 per cent of the personal scale rate of supplementary benefit for up to 6 weeks (though his dependents' benefits and rent are paid in full). If the person continues to refuse work, he can be required to attend a re-establishment centre as a condition for getting supplementary benefit, and eventually he can be prosecuted for failing to maintain himself and his family. Prosecutions raise obvious difficulties and the number of prosecutions has fallen from around 100 a year in the sixties to under 10.

So what explains the trends shown in the Table? They probably reflect, above all, profound changes in social attitudes towards people receiving public money. The most glaring example of this has been the altogether new phenomenon in the 1970s of large numbers of full-time students on vacation receiving benefits designed for the 'unemployed'.

TABLE 2
Harassment of the work-shy[30]

	Unemployed people refusing suitable employment or 'neglecting to avail'		(3) Number of unemployed people placed by Employment Service (thousands)
	(1) Number referred to Insurance Officer	(2) Percentage of Col. (1) denied benefit	
1968	28,300	78	1,450
1969	25,500	78	1,440
1970	24,200	79	1,380
1971	19,600	79	1,250
1972	20,700	79	1,400
1973	18,900	83	1,490
1974	13,200	81	1,430
1975	6,900	75	1,220
1976	5,600	68	1,390
1977	8,400	69	1,480
1978	7,700	64	1,630

But in addition there has been an interesting set of institutional changes in Britain since 1973 which may have further encouraged the tendencies at work.

In 1973 the employment service was completely restructured in three main ways. Until then it operated from labour exchanges where the matching of workers and jobs was done at one desk and benefit was paid out at another desk. From 1973 onwards the two functions were split into different buildings, often far apart. In this way the employment service hoped to escape the dole-queue image and attract more jobs, by moving progressively into job centres on high street sites.

In addition the old process whereby an employment adviser matched person to job was supplemented by a new self-service system. All jobs were now advertised on open stands, and a half of all job centre placements were made as a result of the self-selection of a job by the job-seeker. An unemployed person rarely needed to visit the job centre unless he wanted to. He signed on once a fortnight at the benefit office. Until recently he needed to register at the job centre when he first became unemployed, and thereafter only if he wanted to scan the boards or was summoned because he was to be submitted to a vacancy (which mainly occurs when vacancies are hard to fill). Now even the obligation to register has been abolished.

Thirdly, the objectives of the service were changed. The idea now is to maximize the number of placements, with little separate concern for *who* is placed in the jobs. And the performance of offices is largely judged on their success in attracting and filling vacancies rather than on getting unemployed people off the register. The argument behind this change is that the labour market in general is imperfect and the public employment service should try to expand its activity at all levels of the market.

One should not make too much of the effects of this reorganization, but it is easy to see that it could have reduced pressure on the unemployed to become re-employed. I do not think it explains more than a smallish fraction of the rise in unemployment.

The laxer work test has been much more important. The Thatcher government has naturally been worried about this, and the issue has recently been reviewed by an official 'Rayner' committee.[31] They concluded that it was best to accept that the job centres were going to play no role in future in putting pressure on the unemployed, but that pressure should be exercised by increasing the number of unemployment review officers, who are based at the benefit offices and look into individual cases of long-standing unemployment. They also proposed administering a formal test of availability for work before beginning to pay benefit to anyone. They recommend more anti-fraud work, since they believe (on the basis of rather limited evidence) that at least 8 per cent of those on benefit have undisclosed work (often of course part-time), while 16 per cent are not seeking work. Finally they confirm the lax public attitude to benefit. A sample of the unemployed were asked whether 'a married woman who decided to stay at home with her children rather than work would be likely to get unemployment benefit'. A quarter said yes, whereas the correct answer is naturally no.

THE CAUSES OF LONG-TERM SLACK IN THE LABOUR MARKET

Thus a major part of the long-run increase in unemployment is due to a supply-side increase in the number of work-shy unemployed. But in addition, as I have shown, there has been a long-run fall in available vacancies, reflecting a parallel increase in the number of *work-hungry* unemployed. Why does it now require a slacker labour market to contain inflation?

We get a clue if we look for the main changes that have happened in the world economy since 1973.[32] There are two, First there has been a fall in the rate of productivity growth of about 1½ percentage points a year in Britain and 2 percertage points in the EEC as a whole. Taken cumulatively since 1973 this gives us a level of productivity in 1982 that is 12–16 per cent lower than it would have been without this slowdown. Second, there have been two adverse moves in European import prices (relative to domestic prices) associated with the two oil shocks – which have reversed the previous steady improvement in terms of trade that occurred up to 1973. Due to these two reasons, the feasible growth rate of real wages at a given level of employment has fallen in Britain by 2½ percentage points per annum.

Why would this cause an increase in labour slack? There could be a simple mechanism. Suppose that, at the old NAIRU, workers continued to insist on a settlement which (if their price expectations were correct) would give them the same rate of growth of real income as before. We know that this real rate of income growth can no longer be delivered. So either workers' price expectations have to be falsified by unanticipated inflation (which cannot go on for ever), or unemployment has to rise to tame their aspirations for real wage growth. Thus the NAIRU goes up. In the process the actual real wage will have risen relative to the level of productivity (at a given level of employment). But this (much criticized by politicians) is only a symptom of the problem. The underlying problem is that the *aspirations* for real growth at the old NAIRU were too high. The only way to cut down the aspirations was to let unemployment rise.

The required increase in unemployment can be computed by asking how much extra unemployment would be needed to make workers accept a 2½ per cent slower growth rate in real wages. From Table 1 (on p. 8) we can see that 1 per cent extra unemployment produces a 1½ per cent lower wage growth. So, to achieve a 2½ per cent lower wage growth, we would need roughly 1½ per cent extra unemployment. This is about the same as the margin of additional slack we identified earlier as having appeared in the late 1970s.

Finally we should dispose of two alternative theories of

why unemployment has risen. One is that it is due to a *high* rate of productivity growth. Of course labour-saving investment is going on (robots in British Leyland, etc.), but the rate of this labour-saving investment is not abnormally high — rather the reverse. This is why the rate of productivity growth was so low between 1973 and 1979, and why the level of productivity in 1982 is still below its 1973–79 trend (the only reason for the high growth since 1980–81 is the fall in productivity between 1979 and 1980) — see Chart 6. It is just possible that we shall in future be hit sideways by the chip, but the automation scare has continually recurred and been falsified. This is because inventions which reduce prices (for given wages) raise real purchasing power, which makes it possible to sell *more* output — not just the same amount of output produced by fewer workers. Interestingly, the industries in which employment has risen most tend to be those with the most rapid productivity growth, like electronics. If our problem is excessive aspirations for real wage growth relative to productivity, any extra productivity produced by the chip would eventually help to lift us off the hook.

A second rival theory of why unemployment has risen in the late 1970s has been put forward by Professor Minford.[33] This is that it reflects a rise in union power, as measured by the growth in union membership. This is alleged to have reduced employment in the union sector, pushing more workers into the non-union sector. This in turn has so depressed non-union wages that fewer workers are willing to work.

This theory does not really hold water. It implies that the excess of trade-union wages over non-trade-union wages has increased in a way for which there is no evidence since 1973.[34] And it implies massive falls in the real wages of non-trade-unionists for which again there is no evidence. It does not explain why vacancies for non-unionized workers have dried up as much as vacancies for unionized workers.[35] And, most remarkably, it implies that a 1 percentage point increase in

Chart 6
Productivity per worker[36]

The long-run rate of productivity growth has been much
lower since 1973. In 1980 productivity fell sharply and by
Autumn 1981 was only up to its previous peak (in 1979).

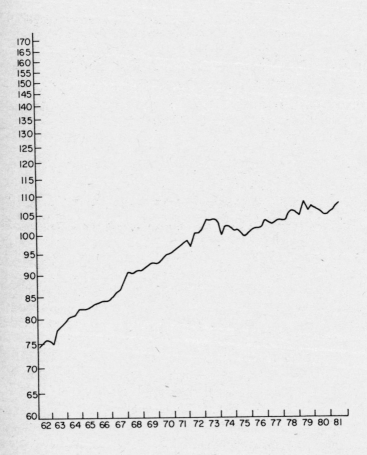

the unionization rate will increase unemployment by 1 percentage point. One can see how this is estimated – the unionization rate and the unemployment rate have both increased by about the same number of points since 1973. But the first could only have caused the second if all sorts of things had happened which did not happen. I conclude that although union power is an important cause of our problems, there is no evidence that increases in union power explain why our problem has got worse.

So we are left with our explanation that the problem has been one of excessive aspirations for real wage growth. In Chapter 7 we shall see how a counter-inflation tax would reduce real wages (relative to productivity) and thus increase employment. But first we must look at the counter-inflation policies of the last two governments.

6

Tory and Labour Counter-Inflation Policies

Both the last two governments have had policies against inflation. The Tory policy has been deflation and unemployment; the Labour policy was an incomes policy. The aim of the Tory policy is to reduce inflation: once inflation is reduced it will be contained by letting unemployment settle at the safe level (NAIRU). The aim of the Labour incomes policy was originally to reduce inflation, but the government came to realize that it needed a permanent incomes policy to reduce the NAIRU. However it was in the nature of a bureaucratic incomes policy that it could not be made to stick permanently.

THE COSTS OF HIGH INFLATION

Before analysing the costs of these two policies, let me say that there are major benefits to be got by reducing inflation. This is not because low inflation is 'good for growth' — there is no evidence of this, if one compares high and low inflation countries. It is because inflation of itself makes people less contented with a given standard of living. There are many reasons for this. Let us consider first countries like Britain, where individual wages are not indexed, and do not therefore rise in line with inflation from month to month or from quarter to quarter. Instead they rise once a year. But prices rise throughout the year. Thus a person's standard of living rises on one day in 365 and falls on the remaining 364. This is not conducive to contentment. More serious, throughout the year other people are getting wage increases. Thus an individual's relative wage increases in one day in 365 and for the rest of the year it is being overtaken. This again breeds resentment and a far greater preoccupation with money than in a situation where relativities change less over the year because the inflation rate is less.[37]

High inflation also imposes economic costs, because a high inflation rate makes the general price level more difficult to forecast. As a result, people make mistakes in setting wages and prices. As we saw on page 24 this leads to frequent oscillations in wage relativities from one year to another. It also makes business planning more difficult.[38]

Wage indexation can reduce these problems but causes others of its own. If there is full indexation there is a danger of explosive inflation. So intense argument develops over the indexation formulae, which can again lead to major unrest (see the examples of Israel and Ireland). Thus under any regime a reduction in inflation is a blessing. But whether it should really be attempted depends on the costs of the chosen method for achieving it.

THATCHER AND THE MONETARIST DOUCHE

In analysing the economic consequences of Mrs Thatcher one must allow for the fact that the whole world is in recession. Since 1979 Western European unemployment has increased by 3 percentage points, as has unemployment in North America. In Britain it has risen by 6 percentage points. The world recession has been caused by the second oil price rise of 1979 plus the non-accommodating policies followed by governments in order to cut the resulting inflation. The British recession has been caused by the same thing plus the additional degree of deflation practised in Britain. Thus one could say that about one half of the rise in unemployment is the Thatcher effect, though some would attribute a part of this to the exchange rate effects of North Sea oil, linked to foot-loose OPEC funds.

Supporting Analysis

The policies are well known. Short-term nominal interest rates have been forced to unprecedented post-war levels and short-term real interest rates have been much higher than has been usual in recent decades.[39] In addition the Budget deficit has been reduced, in spite of the fact that without deliberately restrictive policy decisions it would have increased due to higher payments of unemployment benefits and loss of tax receipts from the recession. It had been hoped by the more optimistic monetarists that a pre-announced Medium Term Financial Strategy to reduce monetary growth and the Budget deficit would quickly be reflected in reduced wage and price inflation rather than in reduced output.[40] But it turned out that inflationary expectations could not be changed in this way. It was only when unemployment really went up that wage inflation really began to fall. The best explanation of what has happened is that wages and prices are sticky, with wages not adjusting at once but only according to the relation displayed in Table 1 (or something similar). By contrast the exchange rate is highly volatile so that when interest rates rise, foreign money pours into Britain raising the exchange rate and making British goods uncompetitive in world markets. Having North Sea oil has not helped in this process.

What benefits and cost have resulted? Inflation, after a shaky start, has been reduced. The government made early blunders, giving massive pay increases in the public sector in 1979/80 and increasing VAT in order to finance cuts in income tax. Contrary to the tenets of monetarism the indirect tax increase passed straight into prices and thence into wages. Eventually the government adopted a formal pay policy for the public sector. But unemployment has been its main weapon and since 1980 this has made a major dent in wage inflation (see Chart 2).

THE COSTS OF DEFLATION

But at what cost? Apart from the current loss of output and satisfaction caused by the current unemployment, there are more long-term effects. The most obvious is the permanent reduction in productive capacity. This comes from the reduced level of investment in plant and machinery, and from the collapse of investment in human capital – the number of apprentices has fallen by a quarter since 1979 and in engineering is now lower than at any time in the last 15 years. On top of this there is the destruction of the organizational structure of business through bankruptcies. Even the vaunted productivity growth is illusory, since productivity is still below its 1973–79 trend. And what would be so wonderful about raising output per worker if this were done mainly by reducing the number of workers rather than increasing the level of output? Present government policy reminds one of the eighteenth century doctor who bled his patient more the worse he got, until the patient eventually died – or changed his doctor. Doubtless in this desert some flowers will bloom. But one is bound to ask if there is not some better way of reducing inflation.

LABOUR AND INCOMES POLICY

When it came to power in 1974 the Labour government also made some disastrous early errors – perhaps more excusable due to its slender parliamentary majority. There was a wage explosion reaching a peak of 30 per cent for the 12-monthly rate of wage inflation. But the government's reaction was to introduce an incomes policy. From August 1975–76 there was a ceiling of £6 a week per person (equivalent to 10 per cent growth for a person on average earnings). For August 1976–77 there was a 5 per cent ceiling. These two policies were supported by the TUC, and reserve powers had been prepared for use should settlements not follow the policy; in any case employers were legally not allowed to pass on into prices any wage increase going beyond the policy. In the event nearly all settlements conformed. The effect of these policies was remarkable, as can be seen from Chart 2 or from Table 3.[41] Whereas wages had increased by 26 per

TABLE 3

Percentage change in average weekly earnings:
prescribed and actual[42]

	Policy	Prescribed	Actual
November 1972 — April 1973	Freeze	0	1.8
April 19773 — November 1973	£1 + 4% (£5 max.)	6.7	10.3
November 1973 — August 1974	£2.25 or 7% (£7 max.) + 'threshold'	13.0	14.9
August 1974 — August 1975	No limit	No limit	25.9
August 1975 — August 1976	£6	10.4	14.3
August 1976 — August 1977	5% (£2.50 min, £4 max.)	4.5	7.3
August 1977 — August 1978	10%	10.0	13.9

cent in the year up to August 1975, they increased by only 7 per cent in the year up to August 1977. Thus it is not surprising that econometric wage equations estimate that in those two years incomes policy reduced inflation by 10 per cent per annum (see note 5). Thanks to this, the government was not forced to deflate the economy, which would have been the only other way to control inflation.

From August 1977 the TUC ceased to provide official support for incomes policy, though it did not support breaches of it. The policy was supported by the sanctions of withdrawal of public contract from employers who did not conform – a sanction that had also applied in 1975–77. The norm for 1977–78 was 10 per cent and for 1978–79 it was 5 per cent, though the government fell (over Scottish devolution) before the year was out. From 1977 onwards more settlements than before directly breached the policy. Some people have argued that as the policy collapsed all the gains that had been achieved in the earlier phase were lost, so that the inflation rate had not in the long run been changed by the policy. It is true that in 1979–80 wage inflation was as high as 20 per cent, but this increase can be explained by increases in prices (due to the appreciation of the pound and the rise in world prices due to the second oil shock) together with the tighter labour market of 1978–79. The best evidence in fact suggests that the 'catch-up' from the collapse of the incomes policy was negligible.[43]

COMPARISON OF COST

Thus there is a sharp contrast between the unemployment/ inflation performances under Labour and under the Conservatives. To summarize this difference we obviously have to take account of the movement of the world economy over the two periods. We can do this by focusing in each period on the difference between UK performance and the performance of OECD countries as a whole. The two key variables are the level of unemployment and the change in

TABLE 4
Labour and Conservative performance compared

This table compares British and OECD unemployment and inflation. Under both governments the change in inflation was similar in Britain to that in the OECD, but the relative unemployment performance was much worse under the Conservatives. The same is true of growth.

Labour

	UK	OECD	UK minus OECD
Unemployment			
Average			
1974 (4th qtr) – 1979 (2nd qtr)	5.1%	5.2%	–0.1%
Price inflation			
Year to 1979 (2nd qtr)	10.3%	8.8%	
Year to 1974 (3rd qtr)	17.0%	13.9%	
Change in inflation	–6.7%	–5.1%	–1.6%
Growth[44]			
Annual GDP growth			
1974 (3rd qtr) – 1979 (2nd qtr)	1.4%	3.3%	–1.9%

Conservative

	UK	OECD	UK minus OECD
Unemployment			
Average			
1979 (3rd qtr) – 1981 (3rd qtr)	7.5%	6.0%	1.6%
Price inflation			
Year to 1981 (3rd qtr)	11.3%	10.1%	
Year to 1979 (2nd qtr)	10.3%	8.8%	
Change in inflation	1.0%	1.3%	–.3%
Growth[44]			
Annual GDP growth			
1979 (2nd qtr) – 1981 (1st qtr)	–2.4%	1.6%	–4.0%

inflation, since broadly speaking the level of unemployment is what induces changes in the rate of inflation. One would therefore expect that, if Britain's level of unemployment worsened relative to OECD's (as it has under the Tories), its inflation performance would improve relative to OECD's. Yet we see from Table 4 that no such thing has happened. Our unemployment has relatively worsened but our inflation performance has not relatively improved.[45]

Why is this? The answer must be that under Labour our inflation performance was helped by the incomes policy. This prop has now been jettisoned. Thus it is not surprising that, although people were depressed by our comparative performance under Labour, they are even more depressed today.

However I do not conclude that we should resort to the fudge-and-mudge type of incomes policy as it was conducted under Labour. It is not really tolerable, as some union leaders have told me they would like, to have periods of increasing inflation under a free-for-all, followed by periods when union leaders come forth to save the nation by supporting a temporary incomes policy. We must be able to find something more sane and steady than that. A counter-inflation tax should do the trick.

7

The Economics of the Counter-Inflation Tax

The aim of the tax is to reduce the safe level of unemployment (or NAIRU). In other words it has to reduce the level of unemployment that will prevail when there is steady (or fully anticipated) inflation. To think about this rigorously, one has to have a definite model of how the labour market works. In practice the labour market is a messy business, but we can understand how the tax works by considering in turn a series of possible worlds each of which embodies elements of reality.

The first world is one where the wage is set by the unions; employers are purely passive. The second is one where the wage is set by the employers, and the workers are passive. And the third allows for bargaining between the two sides. In all these worlds we assume that the scheme is fiscally neutral, in that in aggregate the tax proceeds are handed back to firms by a cut in the rate of employers' National Insurance contributions. This is what makes it possible for the first time to analyse the effects of a tax-based incomes policy in a rigorous micro-economic framework of a general equilibrium kind. The first model I discuss was developed with Richard Jackman, and the second two models are due to Christopher Pissarides.[46] The basic message of this chapter will be that whatever model one uses one gets the common sense result that a tax on wages leads to lower wages: 'Whatever you tax, you reduce.'[47] And this in turn leads to higher employment.

A WORLD WHERE UNIONS SET WAGES

First suppose there is a decentralized union movement. The members of each union face a purely competitive demand curve for their labour – in other words the employers are not organized. Each representative union faces a competitive demand curve for labour in its sector, illustrated as DD in Chart 7. Subject to this constraint it maximizes the real income of its members. This means maximizing the real wage bill in its industry *plus* the income which members who cannot get work in this industry can expect to get elsewhere.

The union does not of course push real wages to the limit because this would reduce employment too severely. The less that a wage push would reduce employment, the more likely the union is to push wages, and the lower the level of employment will be. Thus in the jargon, the less elastic the demand for labour, the lower the chosen level of employment.[48] This is what one would expect. For the monopoly power of the unions depends on the demand curve being inelastic, so that a given wage push does not reduce employment very much. Thus we have established that the greater the monopoly power of the unions, the higher the level of unemployment.

Let us suppose that in the absence of the tax the union chooses point A. How could one now reduce the level of unemployment? Obviously by making the effective demand curve faced by unions more elastic. This is exactly what the counter-inflation tax does. In my proposal the tax on wages over the norm is accompanied by a subsidy on total wages (via a cut in National Insurance contributions). Since the aggregate cost of the subsidy equals the aggregate tax payments, the firm with the average wage increase gets a subsidy equal to the tax. So its cost of labour is unaffected by the tax. But if it were to increase its wage above that level the firm would pay a lot more tax and get little more subsidy. So its labour costs would rise faster than wages rose. This

Chart 7
The labour market in an industry

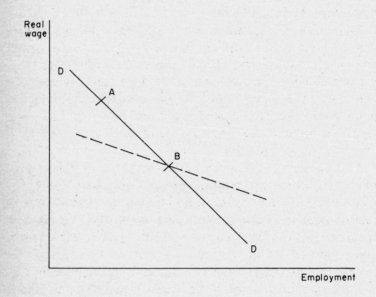

would reduce the demand for labour at high wages. Equally, if the firm paid less than the average wage, it would save a lot on tax and lose little on subsidy. So its labour cost would be reduced faster than wages fell.[49] This would raise the demand for labour at low wages.

Thus tax-based incomes policy, otherwise known as TIP, appropriately enough tips the demand curve – to the dotted line shown in the figure. This reduces the monopoly power of the unions because each time the unions push up wages they push up labour costs faster and hence reduce employment more. So the available trade-off between wages and employment has altered in a way that leads them to choose more employment – at point B.[50]

This model seems to me quite powerful. Unlike many models of union-determined wages, it gives rise to a standard relationship between wage inflation and the general level of unemployment. It also predicts that unemployment will rise if unions hold exaggerated impressions of real wage growth elsewhere in the economy.[51] But the basic point of this model is that a counter-inflation tax works by facing the unions with worse consequences if they raise wages. It thus reduces their monopoly power, but does this by a tax rather than by the thorny route of labour legislation.

A WORLD WHERE FIRMS SET WAGES

Some parts of the labour market are clearly more competitive than others. So we can now consider a world where wages are set by firms, and workers play no part in wage-determination. The lower the real wage the more jobs firms will provide. So how will the tax affect the real wage that firms will choose to pay? Each firm believes that by increasing its wage it can attract more labour. But if there is an increasing tax to be paid by the firm when it increases its wage, it will be less inclined to pay a high wage. The result will be that all firms will end up paying lower wages, and therefore providing more jobs.

A WORLD OF BARGAINING

In many parts of the economy wages are set by bargaining between the two sides. This is of course true in a formal way in most of the economy, but it is also widely true in substance. How could the tax work in this case? It would clearly add to the employers' costs of conceding to a wage claim. In such a situation it is easy to show that the outcome would be a lower real wage, making it profitable for the firm to employ more workers.[52]

CONCLUSION

So, whatever assumptions we make about how the labour market works, we find that the tax has the common sense effect of lowering real wages and thereby increasing employment. For opponents of incomes policy, the mechanism I have been describing might seem to confirm their worst fears. If the only way to reduce unemployment is to have lower real wages, some would say 'Let's keep high unemployment.' However what I have been discussing is a lower real wage *relative* to a given productivity of labour. As I explained in Chapter 2, there is every reason to expect the level of productivity to rise once the tax has made possible a return to fuller employment — and thus boosted investment. In addition even if gross real wages fell, real wages net of tax need not fall, since taxes could be cut.

The tax would reduce the NAIRU. But how would it work in the short-run? As one can see from Table 1, any shift in the NAIRU would reduce the level of inflation at any given level of unemployment. But in addition the formula of the table may be too conservative. This depends on expectations. The table is based on the idea that people's expectations of inflations are based only on past experience. But it is possible that a new counter-inflation policy can reduce inflationary expectations even before inflation changes. This was the hope of the monetarists — they thought that wage bargainers' expectations would be altered by the Medium Term Financial Strategy (MTFS). They were disappointed. A direct policy on wages is more likely to affect expectations than a less direct policy like the MTFS. But, even so, it would be a mistake to expect too much on the expectational front. It is best to just rely on the change in the NAIRU. This gives us lower unemployment in the long-run, and in the short-term a lesser cost of reducing inflation.

8

Should Wages Policy Redistribute Income?

Incomes are far too unequal in Britain. So one of the attractions of incomes policy might be as an instrument of redistribution (and not simply of inflation control). Of course a bureaucratic incomes policy would offer wider scope for altering the structure of pay than a tax-based incomes policy. But even a tax-based incomes policy would have obvious potential. If there were no tax on wage increases for low income workers, one might expect some equalization of wages to result.

But is the equalization of wages the right way in which to equalize *income*? I believe it is not. The proper way to redistribute income is by the system of taxes and benefits, and not by trying to alter the pattern of pre-tax wages.[53]

There are four reasons for this. Let us give them first rather baldly and then expand. First, there is the doubtful relevance of wages policy to the problem of family poverty. It is not true that the workers in the poorest families are mostly low-paid, nor that low-paid workers are mainly in the poorest families. This is because families differ not only in wages but also in their needs and in the number of earners they include. So wages policy could have only a limited impact on inequality.

Second, if the relative wages of the unskilled are raised this will reduce their employment. Those who keep their jobs will gain, but those who lose their jobs will lose.

Third, it is much less easy to alter the pattern of gross pay than one might suppose. For example, the flat-rate incomes policies of the 1970s equalized pay much less than had been expected, because they were breached much more in favour of high-paid than low-paid workers. Supply and demand would have their way.

Finally, central attempts to influence pay are often based on the idea that some national consensus could be reached on what pay structure is fair. This is illusory. One must distinguish here between horizontal and vertical equity. There *is* a reasonably objective test of horizontal equity between two occupations requiring similar basic abilities: relativities are correct if there is no more pressure of people wanting to enter the one occupation than the other. But there is *no* objective test of vertical equity, which could determine what wage differential was fair as between occupations requiring different basic abilities. No series of colloquia or of national commissions will ever achieve a stable consensus on this point. Indeed many people are personally schizophrenic on this issue. I remember vividly hearing the then Chairman of the TUC explain on the radio that the two main objectives for the next pay round should be to raise the relative position of the low-paid and to restore differentials. However, I would personally reject the idea that vertical equity could attach to wages as such rather than to family income in relation to needs. The latter kind of equity can only be achieved by changes in taxes and benefits, which are urgently needed. Meanwhile, efficiency arguments indicate that wages should be settled in the market place.

Let us look at these arguments in turn.

THE RELATION BETWEEN LOW PAY AND POVERTY

How much would the elimination of low pay do to reduce poverty? Table 5 presents the basic evidence. The table relates to workers, full-time and part-time, but excludes people under 21, who raise special issues. It includes both men and women workers. It then shows the pay and welfare levels of the workers concerned. Pay is measured by hourly earnings. The welfare of the worker is measured by the income 'per head' of his or her household; and this in turn is measured by the household's annual net income relative to what it would receive if it were on long-term supplementary benefit. I am not using supplementary benefit here as an absolute poverty standard, but simply as a method of adjusting income for family size. So the table examines how far adult workers on low hourly wages are in poor households and vice versa.

TABLE 5
Poverty and low pay [54]

This table shows how 1,000 typical adult workers are distributed according to their individual pay and the income per head in their household. Income per head is measured by the net income of the worker's household relative to the long-term supplementary benefit level. The table shows that few of the poor are low-paid.

Hourly earnings as a percentage of average male hourly earnings	Income per head as a percentage of long-term supplementary benefit level			
	140% or less	140%–200%	Over 200%	All
Under 45%	20	34	39	93
45% to 65%	28	64	95	187
65% and over	58	194	468	720
All	106	292	602	1,000

The results are rather striking. Nearly 10 per cent of workers earn less than 45 per cent of average male earnings. And just over 10 per cent of workers are in families with income per head below 140 per cent of the supplementary benefit level. But the overlap between the two groups is very low. Only one in five of those in the poorest families (bottom 10 per cent) are among the lowest-paid (bottom 10 per cent).[55] So a policy to raise only the lowest pay would leave most poverty unaffected. This may be why the TUC in 1974 proposed a higher minimum pay target equal to two thirds of average male earnings. But what is striking is that a minimum wage of that level would still leave unaffected over half of the workers in the poorest families.

The reason is that most of those on low hourly wages are married women, and married women workers are not usually in the poorest families. The poorest families are mostly ones in which there are a number of children and only one earner. If that earner is a man he is unlikely to be low-paid, even though the family is poor. For example, of the men workers in the poorest families (bottom 10 per cent) only one third earned below 65 per cent of average male earnings. The other two thirds would have been left unaffected if a minimum had been established at that level.

Thus the only way to deal with family poverty is to have a system of redistribution which starts by looking at family welfare and then gives money where welfare is low. This requires a new major income-related benefit available to working families. This should be simple in structure, consisting of a credit for the parent or parents and additional credits for each child plus a fraction of rent and rates – the whole being subject to a progressive reduction as income rises. Eventually, when the income tax is computerized at the end of the 1980s, this should become paid automatically to the worker in his or her weekly pay packet. This will finally eliminate the problem of claiming and its concomitant stigma and low take-up. By this method we should eventually be able to eliminate family poverty. By contrast, an attack on low pay will leave many of the worst cases unaffected.[56]

THE EMPLOYMENT EFFECTS OF RAISING LOW PAY

Moreover rises in low pay could even create new problems,

by reducing the employment of the groups affected. There is good evidence from the US of the harmful effects of minimum wages on jobs for young people and women.[57] For Britain, where there has never been a minimum wage, there is good evidence of the effect of youth wages on youth employment.[58] This suggests that a 1 per cent increase in youth wages reduces youth employment by something like 1 per cent. If raising wages was the only way to give workers a decent standard of living, one might be willing to tolerate the unemployment risk. But when other measures exist, it seems absurd to take the risk.

HOW EASILY CAN WAGE STRUCTURES BE CHANGED?

However our whole discussion so far is relevant only in so far as wages policy can actually alter the long-term wage distribution. The evidence of the 1972–77 incomes policies is instructive here. Nearly all of these policies were meant to be equalizing, in that they included some lump-sum element – the most obvious case being the £6 a week policy of 1975–76.

What actually happened? The policies, as I have shown, had a sharp effect on the level of inflation. But there was some slippage. Virtually all pay settlements kept to the norms, but the actual payments increased above the norm. Many devices were used – especially regarding existing employees and hiring new employees onto higher scales. And most of this slippage went into ensuring that the better-paid workers got more than they 'should' have got.

Table 6 shows what happened to the distribution of pay. Unfortunately the observations do not match exactly with the incomes policy periods. But we can get some casual insights from a rough inspection, before trying something more sophisticated. Consider for example the change from April 1975 to April 1976. In this period most people should have simply got £6 a week, except for the one third of workers whose settlements fell between April and August 1975. But

what actually happened? The man at the lowest decile got
£7 a week (£1 'extra') and the man at the top decile got £17
a week (£11 'extra'). Clearly the breaches were not equiproportional to income and therefore frustrated the equalizing
intention of the formula.[59]

TABLE 6
The inequality of pay[60]

The lowest decile is the man 10 per cent from the bottom, the lower
quartile the man 25 per cent from the bottom, the median the man half
way up, and so on. The table shows the remarkable stability of the
earnings distribution.

Full-time men aged 21 and over

	Lowest decile	Lower quartile	Median	Upper quartile	Highest decile
£s per week					
1972	20	24	29	38	50
1973	23	27	33	43	55
1974	26	31	38	48	63
1975	35	41	50	63	80
1976	41	49	59	74	97
1977	46	54	65	81	105
1978	51	60	73	92	119
1979	57	67	83	105	134
1980	69	82	101	129	168
1981	78	93	116	150	200
As percentage of the corresponding median					
1972	68	80	100	129	169
1973	68	81	100	128	166
1974	69	81	100	127	164
1975	70	82	100	126	162
1976	70	82	100	125	163
1977	71	83	100	125	162
1978	70	82	100	126	164
1979	69	81	100	126	162
1980	68	81	100	127	166
1981	67	80	100	130	173

TABLE 7

Average weekly earnings in each occupation as percentage of overall average weekly earnings (men)[61]

This table shows how relativities fluctuate but tend to come back towards their long-run average level.

Occupation	1973	1974	1975	1976	1977	1978	1979	1980	1981
All non-manual	115	114	113	114	113	113	111	113	116
All manual	91	91	92	91	91	91	92	90	87
Non-manual									
Professional and related: supporting management and administration	139	139	131	131	132	132	127	135	135
Professional and related: education, welfare and health	121	120	122	127	124	118	112	112	128
Professional and related: science, engineering, technology and similar	121	118	119	115	120	119	118	118	120
Managerial (excluding general management)	119	115	111	112	112	113	113	117	116
Clerical and related	84	86	86	87	85	83	83	83	85
Selling	91	91	89	89	91	92	93	91	89
Security and protective service	101	98	102	102	100	99	103	109	109

Manual

Catering, cleaning, hairdressing and other personal service	72	74	77	76	75	75	73	75	73
Farming, fishing and related	67	75	69	70	70	70	67	70	67
Materials processing (excl. metals)	90	92	89	90	91	90	92	90	88
Making and repairing (excl. metal and electrical)	97	95	91	90	91	90	93	89	87
Processing, making, repairing and related (metal and electrical)	99	98	98	97	98	98	99	96	93
Painting, repetitive assembling, product inspecting, packaging and related	91	90	89	89	90	90	90	87	83
Construction, mining and related not identified elsewhere	93	96	97	93	92	93	93	91	90
Transport operating, materials moving and storing and related	89	89	91	89	90	90	92	89	85
Miscellaneous	82	83	85	87	84	83	84	84	84
All public sector	100	102	106	107	105	102	101	103	105
All private sector	100	99	97	97	98	99	99	98	97

The overall picture from Table 6 is of a remarkably stable structure, despite lump-sum incomes policies and threshold payments. This is confirmed in Table 7 which looks at the movement of occupational differentials. White collar workers did nearly as well as manual workers – and even most of the professional groups did not do badly in relative terms. The popular mythology of course was quite different. This is partly because there were just a few *very* equalizing settlements, especially in engineering, which then produced notorious backlashes from the British Leyland toolmakers and others. But in fact between 1975 and 1977, the inequalities in the wages of workers covered by each particular settlement actually increased for one third of the settlement groups covered by the national agreements listed in the New Earnings Survey. The engineering and mining settlements always receive great attention and it happens that together they account for nearly all the equalization that occurred among 'listed' manual workers over the whole period from 1970 to 1977.[62] Thus among the other two thirds of workers the extent of disequalization almost exactly cancelled out the extent of equalization. I conclude that with few exceptions the forces of supply and demand proved strong enough to get around policies that were explicitly equalizing. (Even the success of Equal Pay legislation does not contradict the proposition that it is difficult to legislate for reduced pay differentials between occupations. Sex is easier to observe than occupation.)

CONSENSUS IS NOT FEASIBLE

Finally I come to the question of consensus. The hope of most advocates of wages policy is that, by detached study and thought, one or both of the following objectives could be achieved:

(i) We should discover how people of the same abilities should be paid in occupations which differ in their attractiveness — roughly speaking the question of horizontal equity between occupations.

(ii) We should discover the appropriate vertical differential between occupations requiring different abilities.

Let me take these in turn. Consider two occupations, A and B, which require the same skill but where occupation A is nastier than occupation B — say sewage-worker and warehouseman. Presumably a fair differential in favour of the sewage-workers would be one which made existing sewage-workers feel as well-off as they would have felt as warehousemen. But in a free society where people choose their jobs, the existing sewage-workers must feel better off than they would as warehousemen, subject to one proviso. The proviso is that they could, if they wanted, get jobs as warehousemen. If some of them had wanted to become warehousemen but could not and became sewage-workers instead, then the sewage-workers' wage was not for them sufficient to compensate for not getting the warehouseman's job at the warehouseman's wage. So the test of whether the differential is fair in the sense defined is whether there is queueing for jobs in either of the markets. If there is queueing in market A only then that occupation is relatively overpaid.[63] And if there is queueing in both markets, then the occupation with the most queueing is relatively overpaid. This is *the* test of horizontal equity.

An alternative approach to the problem is job evaluation. Within a firm there has to be an acceptable institutional mechanism for establishing pay comparabilities, and job evaluation seems often to do the trick. It is of course in a firm not impossible to assemble *at one place* a good deal of relevant information about skill requirements, working conditions and the valuations which workers place on different dimensions of working conditions. But in a country it would be quite impossible to get together in one place even a tiny fraction of the relevant information and 'feel'. So national job evaluation would inevitably involve imposing

on the wage structure the judgements of the job evaluators.
By contrast the queueing test involves using the judgements
of the workers concerned. I prefer the latter.

I turn now to the question of vertical equity. Loosely
speaking a part of the pay differential between skill levels
is a compensating differential (which we have already discussed) and a part of it is a 'rent'. A rent is a payment that
exceeds what is needed to induce a person to supply the
specified type of labour. So why not reduce the rent by
reducing the pre-tax wage? The answer is one of efficiency.
The pre-tax wage has an important function in rationing out
a given supply of workers to their most productive use. If
there are equity objections to the distributional effect of
this (and I have strong objections to it), the right thing is to
modify net incomes by taxes rather than to impose pre-tax
wages that do not clear the labour market.

Any attempt to abandon this objective criterion and to
bring in ethical judgements will lead to the kind of see-saw
we observed in the 1970s. First, in 1975, more equality was
the objective; then, in 1977, the restoration of differentials;
and then in 1978 the low-pay policy. This see-saw itself
added to the havoc already wrought by inflation in inducing
a general obsession over pay.

So I conclude that the best course is to leave the private
sector pay structure to the forces of the market, with public
sector pay being determined along the lines I discuss in the
next chapter. Taxes and benefits should be used to achieve
a good distribution of income. And the counter-inflation tax
should be used to keep down the general level of inflationary
pressure.

9

Alternative Ways to Control Inflation

I have advocated one particular way of dealing with the problem of unemployment and inflation. It is the best that I have heard of. But there may well be something better. The quest for new forms of social institution to control inflation is so important that every possibility should be explored. Many have already been proposed, and I hope this book may even provoke further suggestions.

In this chapter I shall review various ingenious proposals that have already been made, and explain why I prefer a counter-inflation tax. There is not time to consider all the possibilities, and I will confine myself to some of the main schemes being discussed at present.[64]

LERNER'S WAGE INFLATION PERMIT PLAN

The first is a close cousin of a wage inflation tax. This is Abba Lerner's Wage Inflation Permit Plan (WIPP).[65] Under it the government declares a norm for wage growth (say, x per cent per annum). Any firm can now give this increase with impunity. If it wants to give more, it has to buy permits to cover its excess payments. If it wants to pay less than the norm, it can sell permits corresponding to the shortfall in its payments. So there is a market in permits, in which an equilibrium price emerges for them. Since in a market sales equal purchases, it follows that the extent to which the norm is breached will be exactly matched by the extent to which it is fallen short of. Hence, automatically, national wages grow at the rate x per cent.

This brilliant scheme is similar to a counter-inflation tax in the sense that the price of the permits operates just like the tax. But in this case the price is set in the market, while the government sets the growth rate of average wages (x per cent). By contrast, with the counter-inflation tax the government sets the tax rate, and the growth rate of earnings is determined in the market place.

The difficulty with WIPP is to get the market working properly. For the scheme to work it would have to be a criminal offence for the directors of a firm to allow wages to exceed the norm, without covering this by the purchase of permits. But suppose there is an accounting period in which each firm has to be in balance. Firm A has committed itself to a certain wage bill in the last week of the period. It has not yet bought permits to cover that period, expecting that the price of permits might come down. Instead when the week arrives it turns out that all the available permits have been sold. Are the directors to go to jail? This would obviously be impossible. So an adjunct to the scheme would have to include some penal tax on uncovered breaches of the norm. This starts moving us towards a counter-inflation tax.

Another problem with the scheme is that many people would find it obnoxious for firms to be explicitly making income from underpaying their workers. To get round this we could modify the market, so that the government rather than firms sold the permits. Thus the government could announce a norm y (less than x) per cent and then offer to sell permits to the tune of (x−y) per cent of the national wage bill. These could be auctioned off so as to clear the market. This would have the same kind of effect as the inter-firm market. Again it would need to be supported by a penal tax on failure to fulfil.

The scheme has many attractions. But it would be difficult to develop an orderly market. It would also offer trade unions a nice easy target to break, since some employers would have to pay below the norm.

I have the impression that the public would be much less willing to accept such a scheme than a counter-inflation tax.

REAL WAGE INSURANCE SCHEMES

A related incentive proposal is a real wage insurance scheme of the type once proposed by President Carter. Under this arrangement workers in groups which settled for low enough wage growth were to be rewarded by a guarantee that if the general price level rose by more than a certain amount their real incomes would be preserved by tax cuts. This differs from the wage inflation tax in the sense that the reward for good behaviour is uncertain rather than certain. This seems to blunt the strength of the incentive, and introduce unnecessary complications into the minds of bargainers.

An interesting feature of the proposal is that the inducement is offered to workers rather than firms. The reason why this is politically acceptable is that the inducement is in the form of a reward for good behaviour, rather than a tax on bad behaviour. However there are obvious fiscal difficulties in financing the payment of rewards. This is particularly the case where the rewards only get paid if there has already been an inflationary explosion.

THE ELKAN AND LYDALL SCHEMES

I turn now to two schemes that have no incentive features but share the objective of permitting free adjustment of relativities while anchoring the general price level. The first (the Elkan scheme) uses a tax device and the second (the Lydall scheme) an administrative device.

In each case the government chooses a norm for the average growth rate of firms' labour costs. Bargaining proceeds in an unfettered way. Then under the Elkan scheme if it turns out that at the national level wages have risen more than the norm, the government raises general income tax and uses the proceeds to subsidize firms in such a way that their average labour cost is stabilized.[66] The relative labour costs of different enterprises can vary, depending on whether they gave more or less than the average national wage increase. But national labour costs are fixed.

In the Lydall scheme a similar result is achieved by an administrative procedure.[67] All collective bargains are to occur at the same time of year. For a wage to be allowed to increase, there must be a settlement by the 'announced date'. After that date the government calculates the resulting wage bill (q) and compares it with the acceptable wage bill (x). It then decrees that all settlements should be operated at a level equal to the original settlement times x divided by q.

The problem with both these procedures is that wage negotiations get conducted in an atmosphere of very great uncertainty. Negotiators in each industry have to guess the average level of settlement that will prevail elsewhere. Of course they have to do the same thing under present arrangements. But in the present context there are fairly well-defined limits within which the final average of negotiated wages could lie. For next year's prices will be roughly proportional to next year's wages and we know that next year's prices are going to be roughly in line with the growth of the various monetary aggregates. But under the Elkan or Lydall schemes there need be no relation between the average level of negotiated wages and next year's prices. So the average level of negotiated wages will be unanchored and very difficult to forecast. A speculative inflation of settlements could easily develop as negotiators try to ensure that they at least keep up with the going rate. In the final outcome this will not lead to price inflation since under Lydall's scheme all settlements would be knocked down to the multiple x/q, and under Elkan's scheme all employers would be subsidized. But in the meantime terrible mistakes could be made about relative wages, causing massive discontent and economic inefficiency. In addition considerable frustration would be generated when each group found that its final take-home pay was so much less than the level of gross pay it has negotiated.

The difference between these schemes and the inflation tax is that they do not use the local level of wage increase as the trigger for the taxing (or knocking-down) operation. This is based on the average national wage level. Thus the schemes offer no incentive to moderation in negotiation. Nor is it clear how they would affect the NAIRU, since there is no obvious mechanism by which they would lower real wages and increase profitability.

VALUE-ADDED BASED SCHEMES

By contrast so-called 'value-added schemes' are explicitly designed to protect the profitability of companies and thus to maintain employment. The most common idea is that within each firm wages should be a constant fraction of value-added. But as an incomes policy this is subject to a number of difficulties. First, wages are in general determined *ex ante*, but profit is determined *ex post* — it depends on how sales turn out and what pricing policy seems best. It is difficult to see how wages can be set at the beginning of a year in such a way that anyone can guarantee that they will turn out to be a constant share of value-added. In particular, it usually happens that in slumps the share of wages rises. This is because productivity tends to fall more (relative to trend) than real wages do — due to labour hoarding. This may even be in the interest of firms and workers, since workers have little chance of smoothing their living standards by borrowing and firms can therefore reduce their long-term costs by offering workers stable real wages. But it does mean that if you start your value-added policy in a slump and then reflate the economy, almost any wage increase is going to satisfy the requirements of the policy.

Of course all this would be very different if we had a system of cooperatives, where workers did not have wage contracts but were partners in the enterprise. I would strongly support a move in this direction. But it is going to take a long time, and in the meantime we have to find a way of reducing unemployment in the 1980s.

There are other problems. Suppose the share of value-added remained exactly constant. Though this might maintain employment, there is no reason why it should increase it — that requires a fall in real wages relative to productivity. Moreover suppose a firm is considering a sudden increase in its capital-intensity by some major investment. It will hardly be willing to undertake this unless it can increase its profits relative to its wage bill. There is no way in which one could administratively deduct something from profits to allow for an appropriate return on capital before applying the formula. And in the normal course of economic development one would expect that the wage share would rise in some firms and fall in others, with the overall share being determined by a whole host of influences.

The counter-inflation effect of the scheme would be much less direct than that of the inflation tax. For if wages were pushed up, the regulations could always be satisfied, provided prices too could be pushed up. And the problem of what sanctions to apply is just as severe as with an inflation tax.

THE MEADE SCHEME

This brings us to the most radical proposal of recent years for changing the basis of wage-fixing. In his important recent book, James Meade has advocated what he calls not-quite-compulsory arbitration, linked to a national incomes policy.[68] There would be a centrally determined norm, but if employers and workers could agree they could arrive at whatever figure they liked. However if they could not agree, the settlement would be limited to within, say, three percentage points above and below the norm. The dispute would be referred to a national arbitral body, whose job would be to decide between the final offer of the firm and the final offer of the workers: it could pick only one of the two numbers. (Each number would be first brought to the nearest point within the permitted range on either side of the norm.) In making its choice the arbitral body would be instructed to choose whichever number would lead to the highest level of employment.

The arbitral award would be binding on the employer. It would not be technically binding on workers, but if they struck against the award they would lose many rights. Their family's supplementary benefit would only be paid in the form of a loan repayable by attachment of earnings after the strike, tax refunds would be delayed, and accumulated rights to redundancy payments lost. But most serious, individual workers and union funds would become liable for civil damages.

The first major attraction of the Meade scheme is that it proposes a single arbitral system, rather than the multiplicity of bodies that at present exists. If, as at present, groups A and B have different arbitral procedures, group A's arbitral body may settle A's pay so that it is 5 per cent above B's, and group B's arbitral body may place group B 5 per cent above A. This is a formula for escalating inflation. So one can welcome an integrated arbitration system, whatever one feels about other features of the scheme. A second apparent attraction of the scheme is that it lets employers pay over the odds if they want to (or of course if they can be forced to do so). Thus companies could without penalty raise their relative pay to recruit more labour or to buy out overmanning, which would not be possible under the counter-inflation tax.

But the two basic questions about the scheme are: Is it consistent with the principles of a liberal democracy? Would it work?

Under the scheme most strikes would be illegal in civil law, and a whole range of wages would be prescribed by a central body. Both these features raise considerable philosophical problems — not to mention the volume of bureaucratic work that would be needed to adjudicate effectively in the thousands of cases that would arise.

But the main issue is whether the scheme would work. Let us begin with the private sector. Would employers use it, and if they did could the awards (which would normally be in favour of the employer) be enforced? It is not easy by law to prevent the use of strikes as an ultimate weapon. During the Second World War strikes were illegal but the level of strike activity was very much higher than before or after the war.[69] In most cases the government turned a blind eye. For the same reason in many cases firms would not bring suits, in order to remain on speaking terms with their employees. But in this case the force of the award would be greatly blunted. And even if strikes could be prevented, there are many other ways (like the go-slow) of harassing your employer. So one wonders how far employers would in fact use the machinery of arbitration, if it exposed them to such difficulties without bringing very clear-cut results. If they did not, most wage settlements would proceed just as though there were no incomes policy in force.

The alternative is of course to soften the penalties in order to make the arbitration procedure more widely used, but not then to expect it to be able to perform the role of an incomes policy. This would be my approach to institutional reform. We need further laws to encourage orderly procedures in collective bargaining. Disputes procedures need to be more clearly defined. There is much to be said for legally enforceable contracts, compulsory strike ballots and cooling-off periods before strikes — perhaps with compulsory reference to arbitration (but not binding awards). Measures of this kind could reduce union power and help to promote employment. And the principles of arbitration used in different industries should be better coordinated.

PUBLIC SECTOR POLICY

So much for the private sector. In central and local government, matters are rather different. Here a wage claim is paid for by tax payers rather than by shareholders. As a result in most countries strikes by public servants are illegal. This would probably be going too far in Britain. But the public would certainly support tougher institutional arrangements in the public than the private sector.

The aim is not to reduce the relative pay of public servants, but to control inflation. Thus, for the sake of simplicity, the principle should be that average public sector pay should grow at the same rate as average private sector pay. The question is how to bring this about in an orderly way. The following procedure might work.

(A) During pay negotiations the government aims to ensure that all groups get the 'norm' except when a higher figure is needed because there is a shortage of labour.

(B) If negotiations fail, arbitration follows along lines I will come to shortly.

(C) At the end of the year it is found that private sector pay has grown by y per cent and public sector pay by x per cent. Before next year's negotiations begin, all public servants receive a rise of (y−x) per cent.

We then start again at (A) for the following year. If (y−x) is negative, this negative element is allowed for by smaller offers in next year's phase (A).

The key question is the arbitration machinery. There is very much to be said for having a central arbitral body for the whole public service sector (central and local government), using a uniform set of principles. The simplest principle would be that it should award the norm except where labour shortages indicated more than that. But how could the award be enforced? There is a strong case for using financial penalties on workers or their unions if they struck against the award. The penalties on workers could be collected by attachment of earnings after the return to work, and the penalties on unions would have a major effect on the power of the unions to organize their affairs and pay their officers. If the issues at stake were explained to the public, there is a good chance that these measures would receive massive popular support. Even with popular support, of course, the public servants themselves could disrupt matters in many ways and the whole reform could only work if it were handled in a way that was sensitive as well as firm. The basic sweetener could be the guarantee that the relative pay of the public sector would no longer fall and rise so dramatically as it has — people would know where they stood.

Thus there could be an important role for this type of institutional reform in the public sector. But it is an illusion to suppose that we could ever, by institutional reform alone, simulate a fully competitive labour market in the private sector. This is why we must have a proper incomes policy. Taxes are more acceptable to the public than regulations. This is why we should rely mainly on a tax-based incomes policy. To do so is in keeping with the decentralizing aspirations of our age.

10

Conclusion

The basic argument of this book is very simple. There are only three possible approaches to inflation. One is to continue indefinitely with high unemployment. Another is to botch up a centralized incomes policy on a temporary basis. And the third is to have a permanent decentralized incomes policy, based on the incentive principle. The last offers us new hope. With its aid we could hope to reduce unemployment to something like 5 per cent of the work force. The alternatives are either over 8 per cent unemployment into the indefinite future, or a series of crises as inflation lurches around and old-fashioned incomes policies come and go.

The counter-inflation tax has been criticized on the grounds that it is 'very complicated'. If this is so, the critics should suggest something simpler that can achieve the same result. The scheme is clearly much simpler than any type of traditional incomes policy that could possibly last. For a traditional incomes policy would need an elaborate mechanism for evaluating settlements, and for deciding on appropriate changes in relativities. And even then there would be earnings drift, regrading, and all the dodges for making sure that a control on rates of pay within a grade does not control what people actually receive. Most serious of all the policy would be of an all-or-nothing variety — a change would either be within the rules or outside them. Eventually the rules would be flouted and the government discredited.

By contrast the counter-inflation tax is a simple instrument which requires only one figure per firm — average hourly earnings. And yet this figure incorporates most of the information on which the control of inflation depends. And no compulsion is involved — only a tax to encourage individual agents to adjust their actions to take into account the public interest in providing more jobs. Of course individual firms and workers would always prefer in any given economic climate not to have to bother with the tax, and they will undoubtedly belly-ache against it. But the tax will have worked if it alters the climate — facing firms with more demand and workers with more jobs.

Is the scheme really so complicated, or is it just different? Those who oppose it ought to suggest some other bulwark against inflation which is at least as watertight. If they do not, they are opting for permanently high unemployment. The counter-inflation tax may have its problems, but the benefits will vastly outweigh the costs. As John Pardoe once said, 'The anti-inflation tax is not a good thing, far from it. It is simply the best thing'.[70]

Notes

1. Brown, W. (1980), 'The structure of pay bargaining in Britain', in Blackaby, F. (ed.), *The Future of Pay Bargaining*, NIESR, London: Heinemann.
2. Wallich, H.C. and Weintraub, S. (1971), 'A tax-based incomes policy', *Journal of Economic Issues*, V, 2, June.
3. See for example, Pardoe, J. (1974), *We Can Conquer Inflation*, Liberal Party publication.
4. See for example, Grubb, D., Jackman, R. and Layard, R. (1982), 'Causes of the current stagflation', London School of Economics, Centre for Labour Economics Discussion Paper No. 96, and *Review of Economic Studies*, forthcoming; Wadhwani, S. (1982), 'Wage inflation in the U.K.', London School of Economics, Centre for Labour Economics Discussion Paper No. 132; and Capella, P. and Ormerod, P. (1982), 'Earnings and the pressure of demand in the UK', London School of Economics, Centre for Labour Economics Working Paper No. 402.
5. This is based on the following crude equation which David Grubb and I estimated on annual data for 1960–80. $\dot{w}$ is wage inflation, $\dot{p}_{-1}$ lagged price inflation, U the unemployment rate, T years since 1970 and D an incomes policy dummy for 1976 and 1977.

$$\dot{w} = \dot{p}_{-1} - 1.68U + .0054T - .10D + .095$$
$$\phantom{\dot{w} = \dot{p}_{-1} - 1} (2.0) \quad (2.6) \quad\;\; (4.5)$$

(t-statistics in brackets)

D.W. = 2.03. S.e. = .027. Chow-test compared with 1960–74 is $F(5,12) = 1.66$. An incomes policy catch-up dummy for 1978 and 1979 was insignificant. This equation is broadly consistent with the more sophisticated results of Wadhwani (1982), using quarterly data. To calculate the NAIRU in 1982, we follow the procedures of p. 46. We assume the feasible rate of real wage growth $(\dot{w} - \dot{p})$ is 2 per cent. This gives NAIRU = $(.095 + 12(.0054) - .02)/1.68 = .083$.

6. If $\dot{w}$ is money wage inflation, $\dot{p}^e$ is expected price inflation, u is unemployment and T is the tax rate, the 'Phillips curve' becomes
$$\dot{w} = \dot{p}^e + f(u) - \gamma T$$
The argument in the text assumes that price expectations are formed by an adaptive process based on past experience. However the spirit of the argument would not be altered if one assumed 'rational expectations'.

In the short-run, the tax may also work by affecting $\dot{p}^e$.

7. Capella, P. and Ormerod, P. (1982), 'Earnings and the pressure of demand in the UK', London School of Economics, Centre for Labour Economics Working Paper No. 402. Note also the small number of workers in the public sector with real 'industrial muscle'. As a percentage of the total labour force we have the miners 1.1, electricity workers 0.7, gas workers 0.4, water workers 0.2 and dockers 0.6; 3.0 in total. Note also that in the 4 years 1977–80 strike days per worker were rather lower in the public sector than the private sector. (*Department of Employment Gazette*, July 1981, p. 295.)

8. On the Civil Service see Layard, R., Marin A. and Zabalza, A. (1982), 'Trends in Civil Service pay relative to the private sector', London School of Economics, Centre for Labour Economics Discussion Paper No. 121.

9. This is only so if inflation is stable. Rising inflation would hurt public sector workers and vice versa. Note that in the long-run public and private sector pay do in any case grow at the same rate (*Department of Employment Gazette*, Dec. 1977, pp. 1338–9).

10. Quotation due to Blinder, A.S. (1979), *Economic Policy and the Great Stagflation*, London and New York: Academic Press.

11. Some economists would not agree with this; they would argue that prices are a simple proportionate mark-up on costs. In this case an incomes policy cannot in the medium-run affect the real product wage. In the short-run when wage inflation is reduced prices will go on rising faster than wages at first, but they will then go on decelerating after wage inflation has become stable.

12. To find out whether net real wages would rise we need to know the sign of
$$d\,(W(1-t)) = dW \left(1 - t - W\,\frac{dt}{dW} \right)$$
where t is the general tax rate and W the gross wage rate. Assuming

no change in the budget deficit the government budget constraint is
$tWE - (1-E)B = $ constant
where E is employment and B unemployment benefit. Hence

$$(t + B/W) \frac{dE}{dW} \cdot \frac{W}{E} + t + \frac{dt}{dW} \, W = 0$$

Hence when wages fall, net wages rise if

$$\frac{dE}{dW} \cdot \frac{W}{E} > \frac{1}{t + B/W} = 1$$

Of course if the budget deficit were allowed to rise a less stringent condition would apply.

13. Matthews, R. (1982), 'Comment on "An inflation tax" by Jackman and Layard', *Fiscal Studies*, March.

14. Companies would be defined as for corporation tax.

15. Ashenfelter, O. and Layard, R. (1981), 'Incomes policy and wage differentials', London School of Economics, Centre for Labour Economics Discussion Paper No. 44, and *Economica*, forthcoming.

16. Let E be the number of workers, T the tax rate, $\overline{W}$ the firm's average wage, $\overline{W}_0$ last year's average wage adjusted for the norm, and W the wage of a particular worker. The firm's tax liability if the worker is not hired is $T(\overline{W}-\overline{W}_0)E$ and if the worker *is* hired it is $T(\overline{W}E + W - \overline{W}_0 (E + 1))$. The difference is $T(W - \overline{W}_0)$. Presumably $\overline{W}_0$ is approximately the same as $\overline{W}$.

17. This assumes an effective real discount rate of 10 per cent (allowing for the general uncertainties attaching to the tax).

18. Minford, P. (1982), *Financial Times*, 31 March.

19. This is recommended in Pardoe, J. (1974), *We Can Conquer Inflation*, Liberal Party publication.

20. One could consider a scheme to reward workers by say $\frac{1}{2} (\pi-g)W_0$ where π was some rather high growth rate of wages, g was the actual growth and W_0 was last year's wage. But this would have to be financed by some other tax increase, and the psychological effect of a high point of reference (π) might not be very satisfactory. In addition workers would prefer to earn their income rather than get part of it as a reward for good behaviour.

21. (a) Each observation is an annual average.

    (b) Unemployment: seasonally adjusted, excluding school-leavers.

    (c) Shortage of skilled labour: percentage of firms in manufacturing expecting their output over the next four months to be limited by shortage of skilled labour. (Percentage is weighted by number of employees.) Source: Confederation of British Industries, *Industrial Trends Survey*.

(d) Wage inflation: average weekly earnings, 12-monthly rate of increase.

22. See Nickell, S.J. (1980), 'The determinants of equilibrium unemployment in Britain', London School of Economics, Centre for Labour Economics Discussion Paper No. 78, and *Economic Journal*, forthcoming.

23. (a) Unemployment rate: weighted average of unemployment rate of all EEC countries except Luxembourg and Greece. The weights were 1975 labour force.

(b) Labour shortage: geometric weighted average index of vacancies 1960–81 = 100. Data from Belgium, Germany, Netherlands and UK only. Weights are labour force.

(c) Wage inflation: weighted average of wage inflation rates. Countries as in (a). The weights are 1975 GDP in US dollars.

24. David Grubb and I estimated the following relation between the unemployment rate (U) and the percentage of firms experiencing labour shortage (S) and time (T), using annual data 1960–80.

$$\ln U = -3.26 - .018S + .067T + .0017T^2$$
$$(7.2) \quad (18.2) \quad (2.6)$$

(t-statistics in brackets) DW = 1.10 s.e. = .097
For 1960–69 $\bar{S}$ = 26.4 and for 1975–81 $\bar{S}$ = 14.6.
∴ $\Delta \ln U = -.018$ (11.8). If we evaluate ΔU at the current NAIRU of .08, $\Delta U = -1.7$. Note that if we had regressed S on $\ln U$ we should have got a higher coefficient and a bigger estimated ΔU.

25. For a theoretical analysis of this point and the next two see Jackman, R. and Layard, R. (1980), 'The efficiency case for long-run labour market policies', *Economica*, August.

26. Department of Health and Social Security statistics show that in November 1980, 57% were single, 16% married without children, 19% with 1 or more children and 8% with 3 or more. Of course the relevant issue is the *marginal* structure of unemployment and here it is relevant that the proportion of single people has been rising.

27. Department of Health and Social Security, *Social Security Statistics 1978*.

28. Nickell, S.J. (1979), 'The effect of unemployment and related benefits on the duration of unemployment', *Economic Journal*,

Vol. 89, pp. 34–49. This is in line with the findings of US cross-sectional studies.

29. Source: DHSS. The average earnings of single people are below overall average earnings.

30. Sources: Cols. (1) and (2), Department of Health and Social Security; Col. (3) Manpower Services Commission, mainly from *Job Centres: An Evaluation*, p. 36.

31. Department of Employment and Department of Health and Social Security (1981), *Payment of Benefits to Unemployed People*, March.

32. This argument is based on Grubb, D., Jackman, R. and Layard, R. (1982), 'Causes of the current stagflation', London School of Economics, Centre for Labour Economics Discussion Paper No. 96, and *Review of Economic Studies*, forthcoming.

33. Minford, P. (1981), 'Labour market equilibrium in an open economy', paper presented to the Conference on Unemployment, Cambridge, July.

34. Gregory, M.B. and Thomson, A.W.J. (1981), 'The coverage mark-up, bargaining structure and earnings in Britain, 1973 and 1978', *British Journal of Industrial Relations*, Vol. XIX, March.

35. Under the Minford thesis vacancies should have fallen drastically in the unionized parts of the economy and held up elsewhere. Thus there should be a negative relation between unionization and the change in vacancies. To check on this, I have taken the 18 main occupational groupings in the New Earnings Survey, and recorded for each the proportion of workers whose wages were covered by collective agreements in 1973. Call this variable 'coverage'. I have also recorded the number of vacancies for the occupation in 1973 and 1979. I have then run the regression

Log Vacancies$_{79}$ − Log Vacancies$_{73}$ = a_0 + a_1 Coverage

The results were (s.e.'s in brackets)

$$a_0 = .19 \ (.26)$$
$$a_1 = -.41 \ (.37)$$

$R^2 = .07$ s.e. = .31   DW = 1.7

This relation, though negative, is non-significant.

36. Source: Department of Employment *Gazette*, November 1979 and March 1982. Productivity is GDP per person employed. Excludes extraction of mineral oil and natural gas.

37. For a discussion of the importance of relative income as an influ-

ence on happiness see Layard, R. (1980b), 'Human satisfactions and public policy', *Economic Journal*, Vol. 90, December.

38. I ignore the view that the main cost of inflation is the fact that I (and others) hold an inefficiently low bank balance. I have not noticed this problem.

39. See Buiter, W.H. and Miller, M. (1981), 'The Thatcher experiment: the first two years', *Brookings Papers on Economic Activity*, Vol. 2, pp. 315–81.

40. See for example, Minford, P. and Peel, D. (1981), 'Is the government's economic strategy on course?', *Lloyds Bank Review*, No. 140, April.

41. (a) *Actual earnings.* There is no monthly series which distinguishes between men and women. The table therefore relates to both sexes.

   The data are from the *D. E. Gazette*, May 1978, pp. 633–5 and relate to full-time and part-time workers.

   For the period April–April they can be compared with the results for full-time workers from the New Earnings Survey and the results are similar. For the period October–October they can be compared with the results for full-time manual workers from the 'October survey' and are again similar.

   The earnings data include overtime but this does not distort the picture, as the following numbers show (males only, April–April).

	73/4	74/5	75/6	76/7	77/8
Including overtime	13.8	27.5	18.1	9.5	13.4
Excluding overtime	13.9	29.3	19.0	9.3	13.0

   (b) *Prescribed earnings.* These do not allow for the exceptions to incomes policy allowed where women's pay was increased relative to men's during the approach to Equal Pay. However in fact for full-time workers male weekly earnings grew slightly faster than male-plus-female earnings in each April–April period except from 1974–75 when all workers' pay increased 2.0 percentage points more than men's and in 1973–74 and 1975–76 when the difference was 0.8 percentage points. (The relative pay of women grew considerably, but women account for less than a quarter of all earnings; and women have been an increasing fraction of the workforce, which reduces the overall growth rate of earnings.)

(c) It is approximately correct to think of the policies as beginning and ending on the first of the month, while the actual data are recorded at some date during the month.

42. The definitions are in note 41.

43. Wadhwani, S. (1981), 'Wage inflation in the U.K.', London School of Economics, Centre for Labour Economics Discussion Paper No. 132. The results of Henry and Ormerod (1978) are suspect since they found that higher unemployment led to higher inflation.

44. OECD figures relate to the big seven (USA, Canada, Japan, France, Germany, Italy, UK).

45. It is no answer to say that inflation was increasing when Mrs Thatcher came to office. For so it was when Labour came into office. More importantly the inflation rate is changed by the level of the unemployment rate. There should therefore be a relation between

$$(\dot{p}_{t+n} - \dot{p}_t) \text{ and } \sum_{j=t}^{t+n} U_j$$

where $\dot{p}$ is the rate of inflation and U is the rate of unemployment.

46. Jackman, R. and Layard, R. (1982), 'Trade unions, the NAIRU and a wage-inflation tax', London School of Economics, Centre for Labour Economics Discussion Paper No. 100, and *Economica*, August; and Pissarides, C. (1982), 'The effect of a wage tax on equilibrium unemployment', London School of Economics, Centre for Labour Economics Discussion Paper No. 118.

47. This is only true of course when income effects have been eliminated, as they have by our procedure for ensuring fiscal neutrality.

48. If we assume that ex post workers have to get paid the same wages as they think prevail elsewhere, then unemployment equals $\theta/(\eta - 1 + \theta)$, where η is the elasticity of demand and θ the fraction of workers in an industry hired from outside.

49. This would be so at least until wages fell to the level of the norm. If there was a negative range of tax it would be so for all levels of the wage.

50. Unemployment is now $\theta/(\eta (1 + (\delta - g) t) - 1 + \theta)$ where t is the tax rate on wage growth, δ is the union's discount rate, and g is productivity growth.

51. This may explain why unemployment has increased since the fall in actual real wage growth discussed in Chapter 5.

52. For another bargaining model see Nickell, S.J. (1981), 'Some notes

on a bargaining model of the Phillips curve', London School of Economics, Centre for Labour Economics Working Paper No. 338.

53. The argument of this chapter is based on Layard, R. (1980a), 'Wages policy and the redistribution of income', in D. Collard, R. Lecomber and M. Slater (eds), *Income Distribution: The Limits to Redistribution*, Colston Society, 1980.

54. (a) Excludes people under 21 or over pensionable age.
    (b) Housing costs are deducted from net income and also excluded from SB.
       Source: General Household Survey tapes as used in Layard, R., Piachaud, D. and Stewart, M. (1978), *The Causes of Poverty*, Background Paper No. 5, Royal Commission for the Distribution of Income and Wealth, London: HMSO, Data relate to 1975.

55. The correlation between the two variables is 0.27. See also Layard, R. and Zabalza, A. (1979), 'Family income distribution: explanation and policy evaluation', *Journal of Political Economy*, Special Issue, October.

56. For further analysis of minimum wage changes and income distribution see Piachaud, D. (1981), 'The distribution and redistribution of incomes', London School of Economics, Centre for Labour Economics, Working Paper No. 301.

57. Hamermesh, D. (1981), 'Minimum wages and the demand for labor', National Bureau of Economic Research Working Paper No. 656.

58. Abowd, J., Layard, R. and Nickell, S.J. (1980), 'The demand for labour by age and sex', London School of Economics, Centre for Labour Economics Working Paper No. 110 (2nd revision), and Hutchinson, G., Barr, N.A. and Drobny, A. (1979), 'A sequential approach to the dynamic specification of the demand for young male labour in Great Britain', Queen Mary College, Department of Economics Working Paper No. 60.

59. We can investigate the question rather more systematically by performing the following experiment. Suppose that within some period there is a formula giving a fixed sum with or without a percentage element. If we know the overall average increase in wages which occurred, we can calculate a predicted wage in the second period for each percentile group on the assumption that the breaches of the policy were equiproportional to income, i.e.

that the equalizing effect of the formula was more or less achieved. If we then express the percentile wage as a percentage of the median, this percentage must be predicted to rise for percentiles below the median, and to fall for percentiles above the median. In fact, between April 1975 and April 1977 the lower decile relative to the median should have risen by 2.7 percentage points as a result of the £6 a week. But it actually rose by only 1.0 percentage points. The upper decile relative to the median should have fallen by 5.5 percentage points, and in fact did not change. Thus the £6 a week had a very small equalizing effect. By contrast, the more modest £1 lump-sum of the Heath period does seem to have had the predicted effects on wage structure between April 1973 and April 1974. (See Ashenfelter, O. and Layard, R. (1981), 'Incomes policy and wage differentials', London School of Economics, Centre for Labour Economics Discussion Paper No. 44, and *Economica*, forthcoming.)

60. The table relates to the gross weekly earnings net of overtime of those whose pay was not affected by absence. The pay period included one particular date in April and lasted one week for most weekly-paid workers and one month for most monthly-paid workers. Source: Department of Employment *New Earnings Survey*.

61. The table relates to full-time men aged 21 and over whose pay was not affected by absence. Data relate to April.

62. I refer to the contribution of the within-group variance in these two groups to the fall in variance of log hourly earnings among male manual workers covered by agreements listed in the New Earnings Survey.

63. Not a bad test of queueing for a job is the proportion of new entrants whose fathers or uncles were in the occupation (at any rate among jobs in conurbations).

64. For a survey of possible schemes see Fogarty, M.P. (1973). 'Fiscal measures and wage settlements', *British Journal of Industrial Relations*, Vol. XI, March; and Blackaby, F. (1981), *The Reform of the Pay Bargaining System*, NIESR, Chapter 4. For the recent American debate see *Brookings Papers on Economic Activity*, 1978, 2.

65. Lerner, A. (1978), 'A wage-increase permit plan to stop inflation', *Brookings Papers on Economic Activity*, No. 2. His later scheme MAP (Lerner, A. and Colander, D. (1980), *MAP: A market anti-*

inflation plan, New York and London: Harcourt Brace Jovanovich) aims to control prices rather than wages. But in a world of organized labour a scheme to control prices and not wages has no chance of getting off to a viable start.

66. As reported in Blackaby, F. (1981), *The Reform of the Pay Bargaining System*, NIESR, Chapter 4.
67. Lydall, H. (1980), 'A new wage system', *Oxford Bulletin of Economics and Statistics*, forthcoming.
68. Meade, J. (1982), *Stagflation Volume I: Wage-Fixing*, London: Allen & Unwin.
69. Department of Employment, *British Labour Statistics, Historical Abstract*.
70. Pardoe, J. (1974), *We Can Conquer Inflation*, Liberal Party publication.

Bibliography

Abowd, J., Layard, R. and Nickell, S.J. (1980), 'The demand for labour by age and sex', London School of Economics, Centre for Labour Economics Working Paper No. 110 (2nd revision).

Ashenfelter, O. and Layard, R. (1981), 'Incomes policy and wage differentials', London School of Economics, Centre for Labour Economics Discussion Paper No. 44, and *Economica*, forthcoming.

Blackaby, F. (1981), *The Reform of the Pay Bargaining System*, NIESR.

Blinder, A.S. (1979), *Economic Policy and the Great Stagflation*, London and New York: Academic Press.

Brown, W. (1980), 'The structure of pay bargaining in Britain', in Blackaby, F. (ed.), *The Future of Pay Bargaining*, NIESR, London: Heinemann.

Buiter, W.H. and Miller, M. (1981), 'The Thatcher experiment: the first two years', *Brookings Papers on Economic Activity*, Vol. 2, pp. 315–81.

Capella, P. and Ormerod, P. (1982), 'Earnings and the pressure of demand in the UK', London School of Economics, Centre for Labour Economics Working Paper No. 402.

Department of Employment and Department of Health and Social Security (1981), *Payment of Benefits to Unemployed People*, March.

Fogarty, M.P. (1973), 'Fiscal measures and wage settlements', *British Journal of Industrial Relations*, Vol. XI, March.

Gregory, M.B. and Thomson, A.W.J. (1981), 'The coverage mark-up, bargaining structure and earnings in Britain, 1973 and 1978', *British Journal of Industrial Relations*, Vol. XIX, March.

Grubb, D., Jackman, R. and Layard, R. (1982), 'Causes of the current stagflation', London School of Economics, Centre for Labour Economics Discussion Paper No. 96, and *Review of Economic Studies*, forthcoming.

Hamermesh, D. (1981), 'Minimum wages and the demand for labor', National Bureau of Economic Research Working Paper No. 656.

Henry, B. and Ormerod, P. (1978), 'Incomes policy and wage inflation: Empirical evidence for the UK 1961–1977', *National Institute Economic Review*, August.

Hutchinson, G., Barr, N.A. and Drobny, A. (1979), 'A sequential approach to the dynamic specification of the demand for young male labour in Great Britain', Queen Mary College, Department of Economics Working Paper No. 60.

Jackman, R. and Layard, R. (1980), 'The efficiency case for long-run labour market policies', *Economica*, August.

Jackman, R. and Layard, R. (1982), 'Trade unions, the NAIRU and a wage-inflation tax', London School of Economics, Centre for Labour Economics Discussion Paper No. 100, and *Economica*, August.

Layard, R. (1979), 'Costs and benefits of selective employment policies', *British Journal of Industrial Relations*, July.

Layard, R. (1980a), 'Wages policy and the redistribution of income', in D. Collard, R. Lecomber and M. Slater (eds), *Income Distribution: The Limits to Redistribution*, Colston Society, 1980.

Layard, R. (1980b), 'Human satisfactions and public policy', *Economic Journal*, Vol. 90, December.

Layard, R. (1982), 'Is incomes policy the answer to unemployment?', London School of Economics, Centre for Labour Economics Discussion Paper No. 99, and *Economica*, August.

Layard, R., Marin, A. and Zabalza, A. (1982), 'Trends in Civil Service pay relative to the private sector', London School of Economics, Centre for Labour Economics Discussion Paper No. 121.

Layard, R., Piachaud, D. and Stewart, M. (1978), *The Causes of Poverty*, Background Paper No. 5, Royal Commission for the Distribution of Income and Wealth, London: HMSO.

Layard, R. and Zabalza, A. (1979), 'Family income distribution: explanation and policy evaluation', *Journal of Political Economy*, Special Issue, October.

Lerner, A. (1978), 'A wage-increase permit plan to stop inflation', *Brookings Papers on Economic Activity*, No. 2.

Lerner, A. and Colander, D. (1980), *MAP: A market anti-inflation plan*, New York and London: Harcourt Brace Jovanovich.

Lydall, H. (1980), 'A new wage system', *Oxford Bulletin of Economics and Statistics*, forthcoming.

Matthews, R. (1982), 'Comment on "An inflation tax" by Jackman and Layard', *Fiscal Studies*, March.

Meade, J. (1982), *Stagflation Volume I: Wage-Fixing*, London: Allen & Unwin.

Minford, P. (1981), 'Labour market equilibrium in an open economy', paper presented to the Conference on Unemployment, Cambridge, July.

Minford, P. (1982), *Financial Times*, 31 March.

Minford, P. and Peel, D. (1981), 'Is the government's economic strategy on course?', *Lloyds Bank Review*, No. 140, April.

Nickell, S.J. (1979), 'The effect of unemployment and related benefits on the duration of unemployment', *Economic Journal*, Vol. 89, pp. 34–49.

Nickell, S.J. (1980), 'The determinants of equilibrium unemployment in Britain', London School of Economics, Centre for Labour Economics Discussion Paper No. 78, and *Economic Journal*, forthcoming.

Nickell, S.J. (1981), 'Some notes on a bargaining model of the Phillips curve', London School of Economics, Centre for Labour Economics Working Paper No. 338.

Pardoe, J. (1974), *We Can Conquer Inflation*, Liberal Party publication.

Piachaud, D. (1981), 'The distribution and redistribution of incomes', London School of Economics, Centre for Labour Economics Working Paper No. 301.

Pissarides, C. (1982), 'The effect of a wage tax on equilibrium unemployment', London School of Economics, Centre for Labour Economics Discussion Paper No. 118.

Wadhwani, S. (1982), 'Wage inflation in the U.K.', London School of Economics, Centre for Labour Economics Discussion Paper No. 132.

Wallich, H.C. and Weintraub, S. (1971), 'A tax-based incomes policy', *Journal of Economic Issues*, V, 2, June.